Gaspara Stampa

Twayne's World Authors Series

Carlo Golino, Editor of Italian Literature

University of Massachusetts

TWAS 658

CASPARA   STAMPA

Clarior ingenio, forma   *virtutis amore,*
Heroïsque sui   *nulla fuit, nec erit.*

Dan. Ant. Bortoli del.   Felicitas Sartori sculpsit.

Engraving from
Civica Raccolta Bertarelli di Milano

Gaspara Stampa

By Fiora A. Bassanese

University of Wisconsin—Milwaukee

Twayne Publishers • *Boston*

Gaspara Stampa

Fiora A. Bassanese

Copyright ©1982 by G.K. Hall & Company
Published by Twayne Publishers
A Division of G. K. Hall & Company
70 Lincoln Street
Boston, Massachusetts 02111

Book Production by John Amburg
Book Design by Barbara Anderson

Printed on permanent/durable acid-free
paper and bound in The United States of
America.

Library of Congress Cataloging in Publication Data

Bassanese, Fiora A.
    Gaspara Stampa.

    (Twayne's world authors series ; TWAS 658)
    Bibliography: p.137
    Includes index.
    1. Stampa, Gaspara, ca. 1523-ca. 1554—Criticism and
interpretation.   I. Title.   II. Series.
PQ4634.S65B3   851'.4   82-922
ISBN 0-8057-6501-8   AACR2

*To the memory of
my beloved grandmother*

Contents

About the Author

Currently at the University of Wisconsin—Milwaukee, Fiora A. Bassanese was an assistant professor of Italian at Northwestern University in Evanston, Illinois, for seven years. Her teaching has centered mostly on twentieth-century Italian literature and language instruction. She joined the faculty after receiving the Doctor of Philosophy Degree in Italian (1974) from the University of Wisconsin—Madison with a dissertation on Triestino writers between 1900–1918, which she researched in Italy as a Fulbright scholar. Although Ms. Bassanese has published some articles and given a number of papers on modern Italian literature, the Middle Ages, and pedagogy, her main research interest in recent years has been the study of women writers of the Renaissance, particularly Gaspara Stampa.

Preface

Renaissance. The term evokes images of great deeds, astounding men, and immortal artists. When the modifier, Italian, is added most English-speaking people will immediately conjure up wondrous and universally recognized names which, in themselves, denote milestones of human accomplishment. Names like Michelangelo, Raphael, Leonardo, and Titian come to mind. A more informed reader might add some literary figures to the list: Machiavelli, of course; Ariosto and Tasso, perhaps; Castiglione, perchance; and even Cellini. Few would name Gaspara Stampa. Yet, in her own way, she too was a unique product of her times and culture, a child of the high Venetian Renaissance of the sixteenth century, probably the best woman writer of her era, and quite possibly the best woman poet of all Italian literature to date. Occasionally ignored and often misrepresented by the literary critics of her native land, she is virtually unknown in this country, a deficiency this book seeks to remedy in part by introducing this fascinating figure to the English-speaking public. Stampa's collection of lyric poetry, the *Rime*, offers a rich and varied taste of the prosody, motifs, and language favored by her century.

Gaspara Stampa is a poet of the Renaissance and her *Rime* are a reflection of its taste. Working within the structures—and strictures— of tradition, Stampa sought to accommodate herself to the poetic vision of her period. She was a *petrarchista* in an age which gloried in imitation. Neither a devoted follower of Cardinal Bembo nor a true Platonist, there are nonetheless traces of both Bembismo and Platonism in her works. A relatively untrained poet, she nonetheless shared her contemporaries' concern with form, technique, decorum, and style, often to the detriment of originality and at the expense of experimentation. This book will explore Stampa's relationship to her culture, not only as a poet, but also as one of a number of women who developed refined and vigorous artistic skills within the framework of a predominantly masculine culture. Integrating its values and expectations into her own view of art and reality, she nevertheless altered poetic tradition by very consciously interpreting it through a feminine perspective. It is this perspective which distinguishes Stampa from many other Renaissance poets, adding to her unique artistic personality. This study will also examine the various thematic, stylistic, and linguistic elements that give Stampa's poetry its unusual flavor, separating it from that of other sixteenth-century writers.

No work on Gaspara Stampa would be complete without the presentation and appraisal of a unique critical phenomenon: the creation of a legendary biographical woman to accompany or even substitute the reading of the *Rime*. Few writers have fallen prey to such adamant biographical inquiry as has Gaspara Stampa. Her life became the subject of literary battles, novels, dramas, and historical debate, detouring the public from an open and objective reading of the poetry. It is my hope that this small volume will serve to reroute its perusers back to the main road: the appreciation of a valuable work of art.

There are few published translations of Stampa's poetry in modern accurate English. Therefore, to be fair to both the text and the reader, I have kept longer passages in the original Italian accompanied by my own prose translations in order to correctly render the meaning of the selections while also attempting to present some notion of the rhythm and tone of the poems. Brief excerpts will be given in English prose unless the original is required for clarification or contextual sense.

Fiora A. Bassanese

University of Wisconsin—Milwaukee

Chronology

ca. 1523	Gaspara Stampa is born in Padua, daughter of Bartolomeo and Cecilia. Exact date of birth is unknown, but could be as late as 1525.
1531	The family moves to Venice after the father's death.
ca. 1540	The Stampa house is opened as a *ridotto,* or salon, where artists, men of letters, students, musicians, and some patricians congregate to converse, discuss literature, and listen to music.
1544	While a student at the University of Padua, Gaspara's brother Baldassare dies in the early months of the year.
1545	Francesco Sansovino dedicates a number of his short publications to Gaspara.
1548–1549	Gaspara meets Count Collaltino di Collalto, a feudal nobleman from the Friuli region, probably in a *ridotto.* The affair marks the beginning of her poetic career. Sometime during the summer of 1549, Gaspara Stampa gathers some of her poems in a small *canzoniere* and sends them to her beloved.
1551	Stampa is making a name for herself as a poet.
1553	Three of Stampa's sonnets are published in an anthology of modern poets titled *Il sesto libro delle rime di diversi eccellenti autori,* the only publication of her poetry to appear during her lifetime. She is in the process of assembling and revising her *canzoniere.*
1554	On April 23, Gaspara Stampa dies after a brief illness. Some months after the poet's death, her sister Cassandra publishes her poetry, the *Rime,* with the aid of Giorgio Benzone.

1738   Luisa Bergalli, at the request of Count Antonio Rambaldo di Collalto, reissues the *Rime*.

1913   Abdelkader Salza publishes his first article on Stampa in the *Giornale storico della letteratura italiana*. In 1913 Salza also publishes a new and improved edition of Stampa's *Rime*, which constitutes the accepted text for any reissuance of the poetry.

Chapter One

Venice

The Environment

The Renaissance was a golden era in Italian civilization, an era during which the peninsula ruled over Europe in matters of culture, art, and refinement. It was only a small percentage of the population who benefited from this splendid flowering. A minority that included the rich, the aristocratic, and the educated discovered the allure of learning, the beauty of the arts, the grace of gentility, the elegance of language. The few who had the necessary leisure time to pursue such interests soon sought to fashion their lives according to established patterns: it was a society that created and attempted to follow models of behavior for art, love, education, marriage, courtesy, language, and even hunting, although the underlying reality was often traversed by struggle, violence, war, crudity, and corruption. It was an era that reveled in opulence, good taste, and urbanity; it was also an era that saw a blossoming of feminine talents, notably in literature. The sixteenth century produced more women writers than any other period in Italian literature save our own. Among them, one name stands out: Gaspara Stampa.

Gaspara Stampa belongs to the unusual category of women writing in a culture dominated by men. Because of this her biography is also a biography of her times, which saw the affirmation of the feminine voice in literature after centuries of silence. Born in Padua sometime after 1523, Stampa's life provides her biographers with a series of unsolved mysteries, illuminated only by a few scant documents, an occasional epistolary or literary mention, and the data gleaned from her poetry. Much must be surmised or must remain mysterious for want of verification. Her family included father Bartolomeo, mother Cecilia, and the siblings Cassandra and Baldassare. The family name is typically Milanese; in fact, it is the surname of a great and famous aristocratic house of the Lombard capital. This coincidence has caused a number of critics to assume that Bartolomeo's family belonged to a younger or impoverished branch of the noble Stampas. A merchant in jewels and gold—then a luxury trade—Gaspara's father owned property in Padua and apparently earned enough to enable his family to live in comfort and permit the private education of the children at home. Bartolomeo certainly shared the tastes of the aristocracy if not their social position. The three young Stampas were introduced at a very early age to the education of the elite: poetry, music, and Latin among other things. It was hardly the type of education generally given to the girls of Bartolomeo's class, but it was not entirely unheard of.

A century earlier, experiments in education had been undertaken by Humanist teachers, particularly Guarino Veronese and Vittorino da Feltre. The latter had taught the children of rich and poor alike at his famous Casa Giocosa in Mantua; this coeducational environment prospered under the enlightened patronage of the Gonzaga family as princes and peasants, boys and girls, all shared in the master's knowledge. Stress was placed on the pursuit of classical studies, including grammar, rhetoric, dialectics, arithmetic, geometry, astronomy, as well as deportment and physical education. Vittorino sought to train universal men, complete individuals whose minds and bodies would be in harmony with nature. His pedagogical theories made no sexual distinctions; his students all received similar instruction. In the sixteenth century, the aristocracy generally accepted this notion and it was common to educate daughters alongside sons. It was felt that a general education was a necessity for girls in order to prepare them for their future roles as women of station, wealth, and leisure. The number of well-educated and even intellectual women grew as the privileged classes began to associate feminine refinement with the knowledge of the classics, philosophy, and Italian letters. Lodovico Dolce's work *Dialogo di M. Lodovico Dolce della institution delle donne*, published in Venice in 1545, suggested a typical curriculum of studies to be pursued by young girls: knowledge of Latin—although Greek might prove too arduous for delicate minds—joined to the reading of Plato, Seneca, Virgil, expurgated Horace, Cicero, as well as assorted historians and moral philosophers. In Italian, Petrarca, Dante, Bembo, Sannazaro, some Speroni, and Castiglione are proposed as suitable texts.[1] Common education led to greater freedom and communication between the sexes, fostering the widespread development of salons. Even convent-bred and home-trained young ladies were often the educated equals of their male counterparts and could actively participate in intellectual discussions and brilliant society conversation. Socially, if not legally, politically, or economically, women were becoming emancipated in certain milieus. Thus, ". . . however restricted and orthodox a view was presented of certain commonly praised virtues in women, these men of the renaissance were ready to derive woman's true greatness and equality with men from her intellectual gifts, her capacity to profit by the study of books, to engage in speculation on high matters, and to invent, the greatest gift of all."[2] But most middle-class daughters were only given sufficient training to assume their roles as wives, mothers, or nuns. Their world was restricted to church and home, husband and offspring.

Bartolomeo Stampa's children were, therefore, given an exceptional if not altogether unique education, which they continued in Venice after their father's premature death, possibly occurring in 1531. In that year, Cecilia had already established residence in the great metropolis, leaving her property in Padua in the hands of a trusted relative. Unlike most young bourgeois girls of Venice, whose education was generally restricted to the rudiments of reading and writing, arithmetic, cooking, and prayers, Gaspara and Cassandra were taught about poetry, mythology, Roman history, art, and music. Both soon demonstrated a particular aptitude for vocal and instrumental musicianship. It has been suggested[3] that Bartolomeo, and then Cecilia, hoped to groom his daughters for the profession of musical *virtuose*, that is, as expert professional singers and accompanists who would perform for the wealthy merchants of Venice or in the courts of Italy, living under the patronage of generous lords and ladies and lovers of the arts. Music and dance were the principal divertissements in social gatherings. Preference was given to the human voice; soloists were accompanied on the lute, or occasionally on the violin or guitar. Songs provided the central entertainment for the soirées, dinners, and musicales of the wealthy and music had a major role in liturgical functions as well. So popular was singing in Venice that even the young girls from convent charity schools performed in public on special occasions.[4] The sixteenth century had a celebrity cult of musicians who made names for themselves by singing or by playing the lute, lyre, viola da gamba, harp, cithern, horn, or trumpet. The demand for professional musicians was high and the single voice was especially valued.[5] The Stampa parents may well have meant their daughters to enter this field, which was both profitable and promising, for it could lead to a suitable marriage arranged by a doting patron and to important connections. At any rate, musical ability was expected of members of good society and became a necessary part of the education of the well-bred Italian. Music was played in the home, on the streets, in convents, academies, and churches, in processions, pageants, *trionfi*, and plays, not to mention popular balls, Carnival festivities, and amorous serenades often sung from mysterious gondolas.

Gaspara and Cassandra were well known among their contemporaries for their exceptional musical skills. Gaspara's voice was especially praised by her acquaintances, as was her technical prowess. Gerolamo Parabosco, the organist at St. Mark's Basilica, wrote of her: "What can I say about that angelic voice, which creates such sweet harmony whenever it strikes the air with its divine sounds . . . save that it infuses spirit and life into the coldest stones, making them weep from overpowering sweetness?" Ortensio Lando defined her an "excellent musician" while the celebrated singer Perissone Cambio termed her a "divine siren," adding that "no woman in the world loves music more than you, nor does any woman master it so exceptionally."[6] Similar praise was directed to Cassandra's singing abilities, although Gaspara appears to have been the most attractive and popular of the two sisters.

In the years following the family's move to Venice, the Stampa children apparently profited from their training and continued their studious pursuits. Baldassare had already become an admired young man and a promising poet at the time of his premature death in the early months of 1544, while he was attending the University of Padua. Her brother's death was in all likelihood the origin of a personal crisis in Gaspara's life, as suggested in a letter directed to her by a certain Suor Angelica Paola, a Milanese nun dedicated to saving young women from the temptations of the world, who urged her to "direct your studies to being very chaste, very humble, very patient, and full of all other holy virtues." This letter also suggests that

Gaspara, then about twenty, had already entered the fascinating world of Venetian high society. She was young but no longer a girl; in a period when women wed between the ages of twelve and seventeen, she was probably considered mature. As a *virtuosa*, or possibly a courtesan, she lived in a world generally closed to young ladies and even to the matrons of her city, for in Venice, more than elsewhere, members of her sex tended to live in seclusion; although the upper classes enjoyed a wide assortment of balls, plays, and society games, most Venetian women did not take an active role in the gay social life, the parties, the *ridotti* ("salons"), and excursions which abounded and gave the city its rakish reputation abroad.

Venice was a city of contrasts, exuding both tolerance and oppression, freedom and conformity. This duality could be immediately perceived. The Venetian patricians and citizens were a sober, even somber, group in their black togas and caps. To this sartorial sedateness must be added a large number of prelates, monks, and nuns whose robes blended in with the black dress worn by widows and by many matrons as well as with the spartan garb of the members of the *scuole grandi* and the various religious confraternities. The total image was one of a grave, quasi-puritanical people, an image that contrasted sharply with the city's magnificent and intricate architecture, its lushly colored art, luxuriant gardens, exotic prostitutes, Oriental merchants, opulent women, bazaars, and incredible wealth. In 1550, Venice's population was about 160,000 souls, making it the second-largest city in Italy. An oligarchic republic, it was ruled by a patriciate who had solidly established its hereditary power at the end of the thirteenth century with the creation of the Golden Book, a volume that listed all the families eligible to serve on the Great Council. The patriciate was not an aristocracy of blood but a mercantile ruling class with jealously guarded privileges. "In order to avoid contamination, they refused to accept new members; they adopted strict rules regarding marriages; and they kept careful birth and marriage records in the famous Golden Books."[7] This powerful but small elitist caste shared the city with a highly diversified urban population. Germans, Greeks, Slavs, Armenians, and Jews represented a fairly large portion of the inhabitants, as well as numerous Italians from both the Venetian *terraferma* and the rest of the peninsula. Often political, intellectual, and religious refugees found sanctuary in tolerant Venice, including such controversial figures and groups as Pietro Aretino, Italian and foreign Protestants, reformers like Pier Paolo Vergerio, and persecuted Catholics like Reginald Pole. The majority of Venetians, however, were devout Catholics; religious organizations thrived, as did churches, convents, and charities. To foreign eyes, Venice rose from the sea, as wondrously mythic as any Atlantis, to astound and captivate. In the words of one of Stampa's contemporaries: "Venice . . . is a wonderful city because of her site, for she is built in the midst of sea-ponds, and is very beautiful because of the many magnificent and sumptuous palaces that have been erected there. And, in my opinion, she is also a very free city, where anyone, from any social rank, can come and go, alone or accompanied, just as he pleases because no one will find fault or speak ill of him."[8]

The married women were very active in church groups, religious confraternities, and charitable organizations, but Venetian ladies were also known for their love of splendor, generally exhibited in their dress, which glittered with gold, brocades, damasks, silks, and jewels. Oriental perfumes were used profusely, as was rouge. Breasts were often displayed and covered by precious gems. Sixteenth-century Italian women wore many rings, bracelets, tiaras, and earrings, studded with pearls, diamonds, garnets, agates, and topazes. Venetian women, of all categories and classes, preferred blond hair, of that particular shade now called Titian blond, and went to great pains to achieve it, bleaching their long tresses with herbs and lotions while sitting under the sun on their roofs and verandas, thus shielded from public view. The fashions changed quickly and feminine rivalry was so heated that the government instituted sumptuary laws regulating dress, forbidding, for example, the use of silver threads in the making of cloth or the employment of pearl buttons. The ladies enjoyed a considerable amount of leisure time in comparison to their less fortunate ancestors; a good part of it was spent in games, the favorite being cards, chess, dice, checkers, and tarot, or in conversation and music. Some patrician women kept salons or drawing rooms, known as *ridotti*, but many if not most matrons did not actively participate in the intellectual or social life of the city, preferring the quiet existence of home and church.

It was not the life favored by Gaspara Stampa. When her children were still adolescents, Cecilia had opened her home as a *ridotto*, inviting the young dandies, intellectuals and pseudointellectuals, musicians, poets, independent women, soldiers and prelates, nobles and foreigners that formed the gay center of Venetian society. Because of their musical talents, Cassandra and Gaspara probably were the drawing card attracting a variety of guests and admirers. The world opened to the Stampas was glittering, elegant, refined, and quite often corrupt. It was a society shaped by the luxury and affluence resulting from Venice's prosperous trade, which brought spices, slaves, gold, silver, glass, silks, damasks, and jewels from the Orient to Europe. Nor was the pleasure-loving, sensual, and indulgent mentality associated with the Middle East ignored; it manifested itself in a love for color, opulence, banquets, and occasionally hedonism. Safe in its lagoon, basking in the riches of its commerce, Venice lay serene and stable, whereas the rest of Italy was enduring domestic chaos and foreign invasions. This stability, alongside the religious and intellectual tolerance and freedom afforded by the city, made her and her domains an attractive mecca for the displaced who sought political sanctuary, freedom of thought, or merely a convenient place to escape from creditors, persecutors, lords, or enemies. All manners of people flowed into the metropolis, finding the haven they were seeking, whether they were the courtesans and prostitutes of Rome escaping the purge of Pope Leo X or the Dukes of Urbino fleeing the wrath of Cesare Borgia's armies. In this human potpourri, the Stampa children found their friends and associates.

The Venetian patriciate—those names included in the Golden Books—numbered only a few thousand, but the numbers of educated and accepted people in society were swelled by the presence of nobles from the *terraferma,* soldiers, scholars, wealthy merchants, artists, prelates, adventurers, musicians, and courtesans. It was an open society, where admission was granted to talent and spirit, as well as blood and money. Education or genius generally meant social acceptance and breeding and signified more than family origins. Baldassare, having both these calling cards, being a student—then a privileged position— and a poet, soon made his friends among the youthful literati of the city, earning the praise of many of them both during his life and after his death.[9] One of these, Francesco Sansovino, son of the great

architect and a professional author and editor in his own right, used
Baldassare as an *exemplum* to admire in his treatise on love,
Ragionamento d'Amore: "... and, to conclude, a lover must have all
those discernments that could be found in the most gentle spirit of the
virtuous Baldassare Stampa, a youth of great promise. . . ."[10] In the
dedication to this booklet, Sansovino offered his work to Gaspara,
partially in memory of her brother, but also to amuse her and provide
a cautionary lesson in love:

> . . . as a keepsake, I am sending you this rough copy, written by me
> as an amusement from more serious letters, so that, through this
> work, you can learn to flee the deceptions that wicked men use
> against innocent and pure maidens like yourself. And with this work
> I will instruct you and counsel you to proceed in your glorious
> studies, fleeing any occasion that could take you from your
> undertaking.

The time was January 1545; it is apparent that Gaspara had continued
with the humanistic education begun as a child, preferring the loftier
matters of "serious letters" to more amusing literary pastimes. The
warning against "wicked men" was not the first, for Suor Angelica
Paola in dutiful monastic fashion had already admonished the
attractive Gaspara to "open your eyes and don't believe any flatterers,
any of those who love you according to the flesh" in order to preserve
"that beautiful honesty that shines in you." But her music and studies
had opened the way into the salons of Venice, the very nests of
iniquity so feared by the holy nun, and Gaspara entered. From
Stampa's own poetry and the letters, verse, and mentions of others we
learn that she was in contact with some of the major intellectuals,
poets, and musicians of her day both in Venice and abroad. Among
them: Girolamo Parabosco, organist in the Basilica and writer, who
dedicated sonnets to "this divine Stampa" and wrote her an ardently
amorous if politely phrased letter praising both the beauty of her voice
and her form in 1545; the distinguished singer Perissone Cambio
dedicated a collection of madrigals to her in 1547, placing himself in
the "numberless throng of those who adore and love her rare virtues
and beauties"; Fortunio Spira, a minor man of letters, instructed her

in the art of prosody; she maintained a literary correspondence with Luigi Alamanni, one of the century's major poets; Sperone Speroni, philosopher, playwright, and intellectual celebrity, frequented her salon; Domenico Venier, originator of the major literary circle in Venice; Girolamo Molin, patrician poet; Trifone Gabriele, the "Socrates" of Venice; Giovanni della Casa, illustrious poet and author of the popular book of etiquette, *Il Galateo*. But the Stampa house was not open to all. Orazio Brunetti, a mediocre young poet, begged admittance by pleading his case in a series of letters addressed to Gaspara. These letters present a vivid picture of the Stampas' *ridotto*. Although her doors "have never been closed to the virtuous," Brunetti felt himself unjustly excluded and thus deprived not only of "your sweet presence" but of "that entertainment I receive when conversing with my friends" as well, for they "all frequent your house." Besides company and conversation, the outsider also missed the "very sweet sounds and very gentle song" heard there, particularly the harmony produced by Gaspara's "angelic voice" when singing Petrarca's famous *canzone* "Chiare, fresche e dolci acque." Conversation, music, poetry. These three pastimes dominated the gatherings of the gallant society of the Cinquecento, whether in the salons of Venice or in the courts throughout Italy.

Intelligent and refined conversation was highly valued; open, urbane, and polished, it revolved around any number of fashionable topics. The sexes met to discuss love, virtue, honor, perfection, and literature, or to tell amusing anecdotes, narrate tales, recite poetry, listen to music, sing, and, on occasion, dance. In the most ordinary of conversations, risqué language and suggestive subjects were not only tolerated, but commonplace, as were word-games, the double-entendre, and frivolity. But society required that the means of expression, if not the content, be presented with grace, bearing, suitable gestures—in short, with good taste. Conversation was valued as an art, to be mastered by all seeking admission to high society. Logically, the center of social intercourse was the drawing room, the table, and the palace halls. Gaspara Stampa's circle met in private homes, often to discuss literary matters. One of the salient features of Venetian intellectual life was the creation of artistic cliques, often centered on one dominant leader, and joined by ties of friendship or shared interests. Domenico

Venier's coterie was one of the most famous, eventually developing into a structured group, the Accademia dei Pellegrini.[11]

This circle's chief interest was poetry, especially the study of Petrarchan literature, viewed through the theories and insights of the century's leading literary expert, Pietro Bembo. Members of this type of *cenacolo* vied with each other in the production of sonnets and other verse, doting on academic discussions. Prosody and stylistics were explored with verve by a crowd of rather pompous and censorious critics who were eruditely informed on the labyrinthian rules of rhetoric and grammar. Such discussions were often preceded or followed by many an aspiring second Petrarca who read his endeavors to the assemblage. The poetry was then criticized or praised according to its conformity to the standards of imitation. The fascinating aspect of such groups was their homogeneity; everyone with an interest in literature or language was freely admitted. Literary discussions often domnated the conversations, but not to the exclusion of other less elevated but equally pleasant pursuits: singing, dancing, parlor games, storytelling, and some flirtation and witty banter with the ladies.

The presence of women at such gatherings was a sign of changing times, but it was also related to the linguistic issues of the day. These *cenacoli* were not a novelty; in fact, academies had flourished in the humanist fifteenth century, continuing to prosper in the sixteenth. Their nature had greatly changed, however. Earlier circles had tended to concentrate on the recovery and reevaluation of the classics. Indeed, at the turn of the century, Venice became the center for hellenistic studies in Italy, due in large measure to the work of Aldus Manutius, the first great printer and bookseller on the peninsula. As part of Aldus's effort to spread the knowledge of the classics he created the Neacademia around 1501; the membership included such famed classical scholars as Erasmus, Pietro Bembo, and the Greek Musurus. Later in the Cinquecento, groups sprung up whose interests were directed to literary and linguistic criticism, such as the setting down of rules for the use of language or the creation of literary models. This shift in interests mirrored a shift from the use of Latin or Greek as the literary tongue to the employment of the vernacular Italian. This resulted in the need to regulate and codify the *volgare*. Venice soon became the hub of this theoretical activity, thanks to the works of a number of influential grammarians and thinkers. "The first critical editions of Dante and Petrarch were printed in Venice in the years 1501-2. The first three works devoted to the study of the *volgare* were G. F. Fortunio's *Regole della Volgar Lingua* of 1516, Nicolò Liburnio's *Vulgari Elegantie* of 1521 and Pietro Bembo's *Prose della Volgar lingua* of which a substantial draft existed in 1512 and which was first published in 1525."[12] This last work, of extreme importance in the formation of a national tongue, was shortly followed by Sperone Speroni's *Dialogo delle lingue* (ca. 1530). All four theoreticians were from the Veneto area and published in Venice, then the printing capital of Italy, if not of all Europe. A new linguistic situation was asserting itself: Italian was coming to the fore as the language of the educated and the intellectual replacing Latin. The vernacular had overcome the prejudices of the classicists; its triumph was also a victory for women. Due to their limited instruction and unfamiliarity with the ancient tongues, women had been limited in their opportunities to participate in any elevated expression of culture. Liberated from these restrictions and better educated, they become active participants in intelligent discussions of philosophy, metaphysics, history, and, in particular, art and literature. The emergence of the female writer in the sixteenth century was made possible to a great extent by the growing acceptance of the *volgare* as a suitable intellectual medium. A small number of exceptional women had been able to distinguish themselves in the Quattrocento, but with great difficulty, emphasizing their very exceptionality. Isotta Nogarola, for example, protested to her teacher Guarino Veronese in the year 1436 that all of Verona sneered at her and described her as an obelisk of brazenness because of her academic pursuits.[13] Gaspara Stampa was more fortunate.

Although the debate on language still dominated many an academic conversation,[14] it was fundamentally resolved in favor of Bembo's suggestions when Gaspara entered the Venetian *ridotti*. In 1545, the city positively teemed with Petrarchan imitators, the principal meeting place being the salon of Domenico Venier. Suffering from paralysis and therefore unable to enter government service or commerce, the typical professions of a Venetian gentleman, Venier devoted his life to scholarship. His salon was the preferred haunt of the better literati of Venice and was frequented by a number of foreigners and several artistically inclined ladies. Conversation gravitated to poetry, poetics, Petrarca, and Petrarchan imitation. In such surroundings, Stampa doubtlessly learned a great deal about versification, meter, rhythm, cadence, imagery, form, and rhyme. Her musical training could only serve her in good stead, for it was the fashion to put poetry to music; all of Petrarca's sonnets were arranged dozens of times for the lute, the guitar, and most often for the human voice. It was also customary to sing one's own compositions and those of friends, accompanied on one or more musical instruments. Other topics of discussion were Platonism in a popularized version, theories of love, mythology, ancient history, comparative governments, and, quite naturally, current events and local gossip. On a lighter note, much of this drawing-room conversation centered on rather mundane if not trivial questions which were put to all the assembled guests for general discussion and debate. The questions themselves were the obvious descendants of those discussed in the medieval courts of love. The similarities are apparent. Was Lucretia justified in committing suicide after her rape? Can love exist without jealousy? Can a man fall in love by hearsay rather than sight? Can a courtesan love selflessly? What did Petrarca's Laura look like? Is a young wife justified in betraying an elderly and possessive mate? Is nobility a quality of the soul or the blood? Such matters were often concluded with the telling of stories. Nor were the ladies and gentlemen of the Renaissance above salaciousness; their tales demonstrate a marked proclivity for bawdiness, eroticism, violence, and gore. Games were also played, often relating to the subjects under investigation, such as the popular "Game of the Blind Men," in which each player had to present the specific circumstances that had caused the loss of his sight because of love. Often the *questioni d'amore* were presented to the group in verse form. One such question-sonnet exists in Stampa's poetry. She asks a friend: "Which is greater, the profit or the loss, that we see the world derive from love?"[15] The question was probably considered at length in her own *ridotto;* nor could it have failed to plague her after her fatal encounter with Count Collaltino di Collalto, the man she was to love passionately for years. It was this love which led her to explore her own soul and discover her poetic muse.

Mars, Venus, and Apollo

Collaltino di Collalto could not fail to captivate many a feminine heart. If not in possession of the delicate grace of an Adonis, he was gifted with the more masculine allure of a poised Mars. His portraits depict a tall, muscular, thin, very blond but energetic Renaissance gentleman-warrior. A noble name, rich estates, a martial reputation, and artistic inclinations no doubt added to his considerable personal charms. The scion of feudal aristocrats from Treviso, part of the Venetian *terraferma* or interior, the count inherited large holdings along the Piave River. Given the family's elevated social position more is known about Collaltino than about the poet who immortalized him in her art. The Collaltos were a prestigious and wealthy family who traced their lineage to the Longobardi; their fiefs included several fortified castles, the largest being Collalto and San Salvatore. The Friuli area of the Venetian domain was one of the few remaining areas where the old feudal forms survived almost intact; the local nobility, including the Collaltos, sought its values in the military code and its pleasures in the hunt, riding, and the exercise of their power over land and tenants.[16] But the family was not provincial; like many Venetian landowners, they divided their time between the more rustic existence of their estates and the cosmopolitan delights of the city. Collaltino his father Manfredi, and brother Vinciguerra all sojourned in Venice for protracted periods, at which time they earned a reputation as generous patrons of the arts and connoisseurs. One old family acquaintance was the famous, or rather infamous, scourge of princes, Pietro Aretino, who preferred to praise rather than defame the generous counts. Contemporary descriptions of Collaltino are not lacking. Francesco Sansovino gives a short but adequate biography, written after the count's death: "Collaltino, son of Manfredi, had an excellent reputation in military affairs: he was at the battle of the Mirandola with Pietro Strozzi for the king of France. He also served the French in the Siena enterprise at the command of 200 mounted soldiers. He was a gracious and courteous knight: a promoter of letters and lover of *virtuosi*." Aretino lauded his maturity; Betussi in his treatise *Il Raverta*, where one also finds a description of Baldassare

Stampa, depicted him as gifted in equal measure with external and internal "most perfect beauties"; in 1544 Ludovico Domenichi, also a friend of Baldassare, dedicated his published poetry to Collaltino for "in all his ways and in his every deed there emanate love, grace and humanity."

At the same time Gaspara Stampa was becoming a familiar sight in the Venetian *ridotti,* Collaltino was following a parallel course whenever Venice could lure him from his fiefs and exploits. They had acquaintances in common, attended similar functions, shared a passion for music, and delighted in literary matters. It was inevitable that the two should meet and that the count, a lover of *virtuosi,* be drawn to the attractive, gifted musician. Their first significant encounter took place in late 1548. Gaspara was then a mature woman in her mid-twenties, having passed the ordinary marriageable age. She had also spent considerable time in the salons, known for their freedom of thought and expression. Collaltino was a frequent visitor at such places, and they probably met in one of the drawing rooms where they discussed music, poetry, and love with their friends. Not long afterwards they initiated a romantic affair which was destined to last for three years. Their relationship then became the subject of literary history, documented in the hundreds of poems Gaspara Stampa dedicated to the man and the love which dominated her personal and poetic life. For, although Stampa had been trained in her musical and literary studies to write poetry and/or set it to music, it was not until she began to love Collaltino di Collalto that she actually devoted herself to writing.

It is highly unlikely that Collaltino possessed any serious intentions nor was it reasonable for Gaspara to cherish any such hopes. Marriages in the sixteenth century were political, economic, and social matches, not romantic attachments. It was typical of the young Venetian patrician to put off matrimony until his thirtieth year or later. In the meantime he enjoyed all the delectations available in a loose and inviting city that offered natives and tourists alike the choice of thousands of prostitutes, courtesans, concubines, and paramours. A full 51 percent of the males from aristocratic families remained unwed, preferring the comforts of the Church or the freedom of celibacy. In addition to the proclivity for bachelorhood there was also the collateral issue of bridal dowries. These were often so exorbitant that the ruling Council of Ten fixed ceilings on the dowry and on wedding and banquet expenses. In a society little inclined to marriage, property and family mattered, not affections. "Except for the very lowest ranks of society, women were inextricably entangled in the concept of prosperity, and their virtue was a marketable commodity. They were secluded from birth to marriage, taught by women and priests, kept constantly under the closest supervision in the home or in the convent." [17] Regrettably, Gaspara Stampa could fill few if any of the marketable requisites: notwithstanding their possible if dubious nobility, the Stampas could not compete in rank with the feudal Collaltos; she was past marriageable age; it is dubious that her dowry was sufficiently rich to lure a landed aristocrat. Nor could Stampa's active participation in the society life of Venice have helped her reputation; nubile young women were generally kept segregated until they wed, to help preserve their honor, and, thereby, desirability. Once married, women enjoyed considerably more freedom but still had to struggle to preserve their good name if they chose to exercise it. Outside the protective shield of home, church, and courts—where they existed—women were on dangerous ground; the literary-artistic milieu was a demi-monde where men roamed freely and unscathed but honest women were extremely vulnerable to scandal, owing largely to the fact that such an environment was frequented by courtesans and mistresses, who mingled naturally with the company.

Upper-class society had indeed been democratized in the Renaissance and opened to the influx of artists, scholars, ordinary citizens, and adventurers of the pen and sword; it was at the center of social life, not at its extremity. The nobility habitually mixed with other classes on a footing of equality, seeking and finding there similarity of culture and intelligence.[18] But this equality was not truly perfect. The nobility mixed, conversed, and possibly loved, but it did not marry outside itself. And while some Venetian patricians wed the daughters of rich citizens to fill their depleted coffers, it was most unusual to marry outside one's caste for love. When such unions took place, the public was often displeased and even scandalized by the event, particularly if the bride showed traces of improper behavior. It was quite acceptable, however, to take a mistress, or even a common-law

wife without incurring society's wrath; a prime example is found in
one of the most venerable figures of the Cinquecento, Cardinal Pietro
Bembo, who lived with his Morosina for twenty-two years, up to the
time of her death.

Gaspara Stampa's affair with Collaltino di Collalto may or may not
have been her first, but it was certainly the great passion of her life.
She threw herself totally into her love for him, a love which was only
partially reciprocated; the earliest sonnets of her collection speak of his
inconstancy, aloofness, lack of warmth, and indifference to her pain
and affection, defects which were initially obliterated by his dominant
qualities:

> Chi vuol conoscer, donne, il mio signore,
> miri un signor di vago e dolce aspetto,
> giovane d'anni e vecchio d'intelletto,
> imagin de la gloria e del valore:
> di pelo biondo, e di vivo colore,
> di persona alta e spazioso petto,
> e finalmente in ogni opra perfetto,
> fuor ch'un poco (oimè lassa!) empio in amore. (VII)

> (Ladies, if you wish to know my lord, gaze upon a
> gentleman of grace and sweet appearance, young in
> years and old in intellect, the picture of glory
> and valor: his hair is blond, his color bright,
> his figure tall, his chest is broad, and, last of
> all, in every deed he's perfect, save that he's
> a bit [alas, poor me!] pitiless in love.)

For Collaltino, their relationship presumably represented little more
than a temporary involvement with an attractive, intelligent, sophisticated, and enamored woman; doubtlessly, his conceit was caressed by
her ardent devotion and the poetry it inspired. For Gaspara, it was a
consuming passion, whose moments and mementos she transformed
into the subject of her art: she and her love, he and his lack of it. It
was an affair characterized by repeated separations when the count
visited his estates or joined the court of King Henri II of France at the

time of his captain Orazio Farnese's marriage to the monarch's illegitimate daughter, staying to fight against the British at Boulogne. He generally ignored the many letters and poems she would send as assurances of her love, fidelity, and servility. Mars and Venus clash in these poems of separation. She resented his military exploits and his search for social recognition for it caused her the pain of solitude and the fear of permanent abandon. As a sign of her devotion, she even assumed a poetic name—Anassilla—in honor of the Latin name of the Piave River, along whose banks his lands lay.

In this mood of humble loyalty and yearning, Gaspara Stampa first collected her poems to send to the recalcitrant Collaltino. About a hundred compositions were accompanied by a letter, for it was then the fashion when publishing or collecting any work in manuscript to add a personal dedication. The letter captures the nature of their rapport and gives an indication of the poetry's content. We can presume that the letter and early *canzoniere* were sent during the summer of 1549.

To My Illustrious Lord

> Since my amorous pangs, which for love of Yr. Ldp. I carry written in various letters and rhymes, have been unable, one by one, to even make you kind enough to write me a word, much less make Yr. Ldp. merciful toward me, I resolved to gather them all in this book, to see if all of them together could make you so. Here, therefore, Yr. Ldp. will discover not the sea of my passions, tears and torments, because it is a bottomless one, but only a small rivulet of them; nor should Yr. Ldp. think that I have done this to make you aware of your cruelty, for it cannot be called cruelty where there is no obligation, nor to afflict you, but rather to acquaint you with your greatness and cheer you. For, seeing these fruits which have issued from your hardness toward me, you will be able to conjecture the nature of those that will issue from your pity. . . . If ever it happen that my poor and melancholy house be made worthy to receive its great guest, namely Yr. Ldp., I'm sure that the beds, the chambers, the halls and everything will narrate the laments, the sobs, the sighs and tears that night and day I've shed, calling Yr. Ldp.'s name, but always blessing heaven and my good fortune in

the midst of my greatest torments for their cause: because it is far
better to die for you, count, than rejoice for anyone else. But what
am I doing? Why am I needlessly keeping Yr. Ldp. and boring
you, insulting even my rhymes, as though they were unable to
present themselves and needed someone else's help?. . .

During her involvement with Collaltino, Gaspara Stampa continued
to frequent the *ridotti,* acquiring a certain standing in the artistic
community. Her love soon became the subject not only of her amorous
poetry, but of her occasional verse as well.[19] Often in poems addressed
to friends and other members of her literary circle she mentioned her
"conte," occasionally requesting her intimates to help her by immor-
talizing him in their own works: Domenico Venier is requested to
describe her count's qualities and her own flame and fidelity (CCLII);
Vinciguerra II di Collalto is asked to intercede for her with his brother
and is thanked for it (CCLVIII); she declares to Girolamo Molin that
she wishes to tell the entire world "the noble cause of my immortal
fire" (CCLX). These correspondence sonnets also hint at her growing
fame, as in CCLXIV, where she declares: "What does it avail me, sir,
to be, as you say, illustrious and celebrated among people, if I feel no
joy within my soul?" A sequence of sonnets (CCLXVII–CCLXX and
CCLXXXIV–CCLXXXV) suggest that Gaspara had also become a
member of an official academy. A number of pastoral images and
names intimates that the group took on pseudonyms reminiscent of the
bucolic world of Sannazaro's *Arcadia.* It was probably at this time that
Stampa began using the name Anassilla, defining herself a "shepherdess of ardent zeal and passionate, inflamed heart." Her companions,
all "celebrated shepherds," apparently spent their time creating elegant
poetry, much of it in honor of each other, for Stampa begs them to
"turn your tongues and words to speak of more eminent and worthy
things than I am, dear and honored company." From the scant
documentation available on such groups, it has been suggested that
Gaspara had participated in the Accademia dei Dubbiosi, or Doubters,
just one of many such clubs to form during the fifteenth and sixteenth
centuries.[20]

In the meantime, her love for Collaltino alternated between periods
of happiness and abandon, longing and dismay, intimacy and separa-

tion. Occasionally, she might join him during his protracted stays on his estates. The rest of his time was spent between visits to Venice— and Gaspara—and excursions into military life. His French outing lasted for about six months; it was followed in 1551 by the French campaign against the Bolognese, in which he fought for the Gallic monarch, and, in 1552, he was taken prisoner when aiding the Sienese. By that time, the relationship was, for all practical purposes, terminated. Having gone through periods of recrimination, jealousy, despair, and indifference, Gaspara Stampa either recognized the futility of their love or accepted Collaltino's will. It was over; Mars had conquered Venus. The conclusion of this love story is not evidenced in the poetry, but appears to have been marked by a period of artistic sterility. It was conceivably succeeded by the composition of the poems of religious contrition which close the *canzoniere*.

Not long afterwards, Gaspara Stampa began to love again, the new love combatting and concurrently fusing with the old. It was a shortlived passion, preserved in a dozen sonnets and in a name which appears in an acrostic poem: Bartolomeo Zen, a descendant of an important patrician family that was listed in the Golden Books. Nothing more is known of their relationship, its nature, or duration. A year or two later the poet died, barely aged thirty. The death certificate was found in the archives of the parish of SS. Gervasio and Protasio in Venice: "April 23, 1554. Madonna Gasparina Stampa, in the house of messer Hieronymo Morosini, who was ill with fever and colic and matrix pains for fifteen days, died on this day."[21] She had not circulated her works except in manuscript among her intimates and literary friends. Only three sonnets had appeared in print during her life as part of a vast collection of poets, titled *Il sesto libro delle rime di diversi eccellenti autori, nuovamente raccolte et mandate in luce* [The Sixth Book of the Rhymes of Various Excellent Authors, Newly Gathered and Brought to Light], published in Venice in 1553.

In death as in life, Stampa found the approbation and praise of her contemporaries. Eulogies and encomiums were de rigueur on such an occasion, but they did express the general sentiment of those surrounding her. In life, her beauty and talents had captivated. Some had praised her in traditional literary terms derived from the Petrarchan and Dantesque models. Others had emphasized the union of beauty and virtuosity, such as Torquato Bembo's statement that the sight and sound of her were equal to the divine and celestial or Leonardo Emo's proclamation of her talents and fame, "a woman praised in every clime." In death, her moral and artistic attributes were depicted. Benedetto Varchi, renowned literary figure of the Cinquecento, likened her brief life to those symbols of beauty which succumb all too quickly: "the deer and raven for a time escape, but the swan soon dies as does the dove." Her friend Ippolita Mirtilla, herself a poet, regretted the loss of her "immaculate beauty," while the German composer Giovanni Lockenburgo set a sonnet to music praising her as a "flower of beauty and virtue." It was at the urging of these literary friends that her entire opus came to be published.

The task was undertaken by her surviving sister. In a letter dated October 13, 1554, Cassandra dedicated the first edition of Gaspara Stampa's *Rime* to "the most illustrious and most reverend Messer Giovanni della Casa," giving the details of the posthumous publication:

> . . . I sought to remove all her things from my sight, so that seeing them and handling them would not renew the very painful memory of her in my soul and, consequently, would not refresh the wounds of so many sorrows, having lost such a valiant sister. And needing and wanting to do the same with these, her rhymes, woven by her partially to exercise her talent, as good as ever found in a woman if I am not deceived by fraternal affection, and partially to express some of her amorous ideas, many gentlemen of great intelligence, who loved her while she lived and have influence over me, have dissuaded me, against my will, from this resolve and forced me to gather together those poems which could be found, showing me that I must not, could not, in order to not disturb my own peace, disturb the glory of my sister by hiding her honored labors. This, then, is the reason why I had them published.[22]

The book appeared in late 1554, edited by Giorgio Benzone for Pietrasanta. It was a collection of all her recovered poetry, accompanied by a number of sonnets in her honor, written before and after her death. The volume was not a great success and Gaspara Stampa slipped into oblivion. Cassandra retired quietly to Padua, where documents show she was still living in 1579. Collaltino di Collalto died in political exile in Mantua, still a young man. The famed musician and poet was forgotten, as was her *canzoniere*. Silence covered them both for nearly two hundred years.

Chapter Two

Fiction and Reality

Legends and Polemics

Few important writers have the fortune, or misfortune, of knowing some fame as living artists, only to be quickly forgotten, and then resurrected at the center of one of the major literary debates of a decade: such a fate awaited Gaspara Stampa in the fancy and scholarship of Italian literati. Soon after her death the *Rime* were quietly forgotten as she too faded from the memory of her friends and admirers. The causes of such speedy neglect are uncertain but easily conjectured: she was only one of scores of Petrarchan poets in the Cinquecento; her readers were few if devoted; her blood was not blue, nor were her intellectual gifts exceptional; she was a powerless woman in a male-dominated culture. And, while some women were remembered through the years, women like Isabella d'Este for her patronage, style, and intelligence, Vittoria Colonna for her high moral standards, Cassandra Fidele for her scholarship, or Lucretia Borgia for her infamous reputation, the young bourgeois poet from Venice could not compete in popularity and recognition with such celebrated names. Gaspara Stampa was soon relegated to the archives of both the libraries and the memory of her city. Nor should such forgetfulness be surprising, for even within her circle of acquaintances her beauty and musical genius had been better acknowledged and appreciated than her literary talents. Indeed, the writer was to lose to the woman again and again through the ensuing centuries.

The fact that Stampa's *Rime* were published in Venice in 1554 is a partial cause for their lack of success. The city was then the European printing capital and the home of the professional writer; men like Aretino and Sansovino made their fortunes as the Renaissance equivalents of journalists, hacks, or scandalmongers. Everything imaginable was published in Venice, from the early inexpensive Aldine classics to volumes of poetry, plays, treatises, debates, history, both

Catholic and Protestant religious works, even the first vernacular version of the Bible. All of Italy sent works to the city's numerous publishing houses or simply paid to have books printed at one or another of well over a hundred presses. During the century, over 15,000 titles were issued in Venice, at an average of 150 a year, not including fliers, brochures, and short works. Generally 400 to 1,000 copies were produced per printing.[1] The single opus of a deceased and relatively unknown poet like Gaspara Stampa was, therefore, unlikely to cause a great stir.

She and her poetry would have fallen into total oblivion had it not been for an ironic twist of fate. While the love for one Collalto had provided the inspiration for Stampa's poetry, the pride of another Collalto resuscitated it. In 1738 Antonio Rambaldo, heir to the family title, decided to reissue the *Rime*, motivated by the desire to glorify the Collalto name. Rather appropriately, the count chose a woman, famous in her own day as a writer and scholar, to undertake the project. Luisa Bergalli, wife of Gaspare Gozzi, proceeded to put together a new edition of the Stampian work, aided by Apostolo Zeno, himself a famous poet and admirer of the *Rime* in an age which had otherwise ignored them.

The 1738 edition was a splendid text which included several illustrations, among them the presumed portraits of Gaspara and Collaltino. Besides Stampa's own poetry, that of Collaltino and Vinciguerra II di Collalto was added, followed by a selection of encomiums written by a number of eighteenth-century Arcadian poets in honor of the three Renaissance figures. The text was introduced by Count Antonio Rambaldo himself, who penned a biographical account of Stampa's life. It is an important passage, for it marks the beginning of the poet's romantic legend:

> She was one of the most extraordinary and excellent women ever produced by benign nature. She learned both the Latin and Greek tongues to marvelous advantage, after which she totally dedicated herself to the most pleasing of the liberal arts, that is, Poetry, which she wrote after the Italian fashion. She produced such marvellous fruits that whoever reads and contemplates her divine rhymes will be forced to confess that she is incomparable in her clever, amorous and tender manner of writing, while also being sustained by the

originality of her graceful and very noble thoughts, expressed with
inventive felicity. She wrote all her *Rime,* with the exception of a
very few, in praise of Collaltino di Collalto, count of Treviso. When
about twenty-six years of age, she fell passionately in love with this
gentleman, who was adorned with many good qualities. It appears
that for three full years she was courteously reciprocated, as can be
gathered in the contents of the *Rime.* She was indeed worthy of his
love for, besides her unique ability to versify, she was gifted with
great beauty and possessed such graceful and kind ways that
whosoever had the opportunity to see her was left with reverence
and love in his heart for her. This happened especially with the
poets and men of letters of her century. She amused herself by
playing the viola and the lute, having total mastery of these
instruments. Stampa began to languish when Count Collaltino,
drawn by the desire for honor, went to France to war for Henri II.
The great solace the count brought Gaspara upon his return to Italy
was of brief duration, for rumors that he was about to marry were
being heard. Humiliated and above all grieved at this news, a few
months later, in the prime of her life, for she was barely thirty, she
died of a cruel and painful sickness. Even today some still believe it
was the effect of poison. This took place around the year 1554.[2]

Antonio Rambaldo added that Gaspara may well have descended from
the noble Milanese family and that the Stampas were definitely a
"genteel and honored" family who possessed the means to support
even their women in "studies and the fine arts." Compiling this
information, the following conclusions were drawn: Gaspara Stampa
had been a noble, educated young lady, richly gifted in spirit, looks,
and talent; Collaltino, cold-hearted and cruel, had betrayed her,
resulting in her untimely death by unnatural causes, possibly by suicide
but probably by murder. The romantic legend was born.

Founded on this somewhat hypothetical and undocumented biographical sketch, the legend grew and prospered. In 1794, an entry in
the *Nuovo Dizionario Istorico*[3] echoed the misinformation included in
the Bergalli edition as factual data, adding some innovative touches of
its own: ". . . she was a Milanese gentlewoman by extraction, and was
highly commended by her contemporaries as a great poet and excellent
musician. . . . This love proved fatal. Since Collaltino had given his
hand to another in marriage, Gaspara conceived such deep sorrow that

it led to her death. . . ." Fiction quickly replaced fact and the theme of death for love—in the very best Romantic tradition!—fascinated the nineteenth century. It was the stuff of melodrama, material suited for a sentimental historical novel set in the corrupt perfidy of Renaissance Venice. One well-known scholar could not resist the temptation: in 1851 Luigi Carrer reprinted what he purported to be the real letters of Gaspara Stampa to her friend Ippolita Mirtilla under the title *Unhappy Love of Gaspara Stampa*. The letters had already appeared in 1838 in *The Seven Gems of Venice,* a series of seven supposedly factual biographies of famous Venetian ladies through the centuries. Carrer insisted upon the veracity of his find; he was believed. Given some knowledge of Stampa's life and times, it is clear that they are the author's inventions due to their inaccuracies, inconsistencies, and literary style. But they do adhere in spirit if not in chronology and tone to the contents of the *Rime.* An embroidery on some of the biographical clues and details provided by the poems, added to Carrer's familiarity with the life of Venice in the Cinquecento, the book is an original if fictitious reconstruction of Stampa's milieu.

This epistolary novel gained widespread readership throughout Italy, for it perfectly captured the tastes of the Romantic public. It was a tale of passionate love, yearning, betrayal, death, and despair, told in flowery prose. One excerpt from the first letter sufficiently reflects the nature and mood of the book. Dated 1552, it discusses Baldassare's ill health and intellectual freedom (an impossibility! He died in 1544, but the author could not resist the temptation to depict fraternal affection and a slow death by consumption—a favorite disease of the times—which foreshadows the heroine's own end) and the first stirrings of her own unhappy love: "A tear now dampens the paper on which I'm writing you, my sweetest Ippolita, a tear wrung from a woeful presage: these intolerable pangs which now afflict my heart, not unmingled with bliss, will all too soon, God only knows how, become unbearable and destitute of any joy." Carrer then skillfully ties these early omens to the changes in Stampa's poetry and its inspiration, thus inserting another theme of much Romantic literature: the union of life and art. An atmosphere of pathetic doom clings to the entire book, appealing to the sentimental tastes of the early and mid-nineteenth century: "I'm no longer the fairy who, with a touch of

her wand, stirred up a marvelous castle, and fountains, and
gardens. . . . The enchantment is someone else's, and I find myself
locked into a magic circle and I have no power to extricate myself."

Carrer's depiction of Gaspara Stampa, the fairy caught in the web
of love, is in accordance with the Romantic archetypes then popular.
Even the employment of the epistolary format had its celebrated
models in Richardson, Goethe, and Foscolo. True to the mold, the
heroine came to an unfortunate and premature end: having lost her
beloved, betrayed and ill, the virginal Gaspara hallucinates about her
unfaithful Collaltino (an allusion to Manzoni's famous heroine,
Ermengarda), even destroying his portrait in her delirium, only to find
peace with God as the end approaches, although vague suggestions are
made of self-induced death through poison.

Carrer's work obtained a wide readership in the 1800s; more
surprisingly, it was generally accepted as a valid document. As late as
1942, Maria Bandini Buti cited some of the book's inaccuracies and
pointed to the "many" letters written by Stampa which were still
extant (only one known letter exists: the dedication to Collaltino) in
her encyclopedic volume, *Poetesse e scrittrici*. Carrer's fictitious letters
and their great success are only an indication of the popularity of
Gaspara Stampa among the Romantics of the nineteenth century.
Plays and narrative poems were dedicated to her, such as Jacopo
Cabianca's drama in verse, *Gaspara Stampa* (1857), and another
three-act play of the same title produced a year later by Giuseppe
Pieri.[4] The public for such works was the same as flocked to see other
historical dramas, a popular genre of the period, particularly those set
in the Middle Ages or Renaissance; in fact, Gaspara had a great deal
in common with another beloved and passionate heroine: Francesca da
Rimini.

The Romantic interpretation of Stampa's biography presented a
sublime creature of innocence and passion. Her life provided a stage
where the drama of love, death, and art was movingly enacted. For a
time, this image of Gaspara Stampa was enshrined on a solid pedestal
but, as is the fate of many idols, her feet were made of clay. The
Romantic Gaspara was toppled under the blows of an unlikely nemesis,
the skillful and dedicated scholar and haunter of archives, Abdelkader
Salza. Professionally discontent with the romanticized version of the

Renaissance poet and the inadequate and uncertain facts surrounding her life, Salza sought documentation, in the best tradition of historical criticism. His conclusions and research were published in 1913, including well over a hundred pages of text, in the *Giornale storico della letteratura italiana*, creating havoc and stirring emotions in their wake. As a result, further historical research was undertaken by both Salza and his critics, both wanting to defend and substantiate their points. Salza's findings were really quite simple, if subversive. Gaspara Stampa was not a young innocent but had been a member of that unique caste of Renaissance women: the courtesan. The critic's proofs were based on a libelous sonnet published after her death, the nature of her acquaintances, the dedication of some works to Stampa which Salza considered unsuitable and salacious literature not meant for nubile young maidens, a witty remark by Sperone Speroni, the letter from the Milanese nun, the presence of more than one lover in her poetry and life, and, finally, the singular freedom of her existence.[5] With these few and rather dubious points, Salza spun an incredible web of suppositions, conjectures, possibilities, probabilities, and guesses. Salza must be thanked for his efforts in rummaging through archives in search of documentation; most of the factual information gathered on Stampa and her circle of acquaintances was the work of this man or the result of his publications. But Salza's conclusions can be debated and were.

Given the seclusion of girls and the restricted life-style of matrons, there was a notable lack of cultured and intelligent women taking an active role in the social gatherings of the Cinquecento. This lack was acutely felt outside the courts and a surrogate for the educated lady was sought. The courtesan filled the void. Generally speaking, the courtesan was a novel type of prostitute who flourished in the Renaissance, particularly in the two cities where there existed a scarcity of available women to participate in the intellectual life of the salons: Rome and Venice. The courtesan filled the demand and supplied a social need for women of some intelligence, wit, beauty, education, and pleasure. Her existence was partially modeled after the Hellenic *hetaerae* and her contemporaries understood her function in such classical terms. The courtesan represented beauty and love devoid of the constraints of propriety and marriage; she offered an alternative to platonic love or pure sexuality. For many she was the personification of an aesthetic ideal, joining physical beauty to finesse, composure, talent, fashion, taste, and wit. Her home was her drawing room, attracting numerous guests, many of whom were more interested in her personality and conversation than in her sexual gifts. She was respected by honest men and women alike; occasionally, she was revered. Her friends included artists, men of learning, statesmen, prelates, and lords. Now and again, her individuality and talents would be such as to forgive her profession and she would enter into respectable unions and take her place in society. This was the case of Caterina da San Celso, who married into the wealthy and noble Ghiringhello family.[6] Considerable distinctions were made among the ladies of pleasure themselves, who differed in class, education, clientele, and price. The grand courtesans were often as educated as the ladies of the nobility, possessed large apartments, servants, grace, manners, and breeding. They were expected to entertain lavishly to please their protectors or maintain their contacts. Some, like the famed Imperia or Tullia d'Aragona, wrote poetry and even treatises on Platonic love, held literary salons, distinguishing themselves for their conversation and musical skills. Many posed for great masters like Titian, Raphael, and Palma. Quite a few openly participated in the social life of their cities, mingling with the nobility, hosting banquets, and providing soirées. Indeed, there was very little to distinguish a courtesan in either speech, manner, or dress from a virtuous wife.

The Venetian prostitutes were noted throughout Italy for their sensuality and pulchritude. The city dominated all of Europe in the number of its courtesans and harlots. For the foreigner, two things were striking about a visit to the great metropolis: the freedom enjoyed by its citizens and the astounding quantity of women of easy virtue. The census of 1509 reported 11,694 prostitutes in a population numbering about 300,000, although the figures may be exaggerated. Two major types appeared in the city: the *cortigiane oneste,* those who rivaled ladies in appearance and life-style, and the *cortigiane di candela,* who lived in brothels, inns, or seamy neighborhoods and often plied their trade in the streets or along the canals. The two groups had little in common. At one time, the "honest" courtesans even protested to the Venetian government that the common prostitutes were using the appellation *cortigiane,* to which they had no right, being no more than whores.[7] The social significance of these great numbers of fallen women can be deduced by the active attempt on the part of the Church and citizenry to lead them back to morality by creating nunneries especially for converted prostitutes, establishing homes for them and also for children threatened with prostitution by family pressures or economic necessity, and by proselytizing through such religious groups as the Zitelle or Soccorso.

That the Venetian courtesan was perceivably no different from the wives and daughters of the patriciate and citizenry is made clear by the sumptuary law of 1543, which forbade any prostitute, no matter how high her rank, from wearing jewels or silks in church or on the street, for one could not "tell the good from the bad." A number of the city's courtesans came from good families, like those of Veronica Franco and possibly Francesca Baffo, and chose to enter the profession.[8] They were not totally ostracized from genteel society but continued to take part in most of the diversions available, especially in the parties, theatrical productions, and carnival celebrations given by the young blades of the city, and were welcome additions to the literary circles of many homes.

The question still remains: Was Gaspara Stampa a courtesan? Possibly. If the definition of *cortegiana* pronounced in Venetian sumptuary law dated February 21, 1543, is indicative of the word's meaning for her contemporaries, Stampa could easily be taken as a member of the world's oldest profession: "by prostitute one means those women who, not being married, have dealings and intercourse with one or more men and also those who, having a husband, do not live with their husbands, but are separated." In another controversial article, published in 1917 and written to defend and substantiate his thesis, Salza extended the acceptable definition of courtesan to include any woman either living with a man or being supported by one or more lovers. But the documentation remains inconclusive and the critic's view so obviously biased that Salza is still being questioned, rejected, and refuted.[9]

Abdelkader Salza typified an era still saturated with Victorian morality. His conclusions tended to view the issue through one uncompromising dimension: any young woman as emancipated, sexually available, and socially liberated as Stampa could only be a courtesan. The other potential option which justified such a life-style would necessarily have included marriage, which gave women relative freedom of movement and entry into the social activities of the upper class. Disconcertingly, Gaspara had no husband, nor any recognizable wealth and position. His conclusions did not change: she was a prostitute, of the highest order, but a prostitute all the same. With his articles, Salza had stirred the proverbial hornets' nest and the buzzing and stinging kept on for many years.

Gaspara Stampa's profession, or lack of it, became a major issue in journals, articles, newspapers, and literary discussions as greater numbers of critics, journalists, literati, and interested parties joined the foray. Some chose to employ Salza's own methodology to fight him. The raids on archives and libraries continued in order to unearth better and conclusive documentation. The best of these historical researchers was Elisa Innocenzi Greggio, whose article on Stampa appeared in 1915 in the *Ateneo Veneto*. Innocenzi Greggio challenged some of Salza's evidence, presented more of her own, and disputed many of the scholar's biased interpretations. Stampa's most ardent paladin was G. A. Cesareo, whose study *Gaspara Stampa, donna e poetessa* (1920) attempted to synthesize all available information, reinterpreting it in light of the poetry. He thus arrived at the old Romantic formula of Stampa the abandoned maiden of class and talent:

> Gaspara Stampa cannot be compared to any other woman in the life of the Cinquecento. She did not marry; but she adores art, belles-lettres, music, learned conversation, and she did not deprive herself of them. Her house is an elegant *ridotto*, where patricians and poets, excellent lute players and priestly philosophers, musicians and ladies gather. The poet is free, frank, joyful, open-minded. (63)
>
> . . . Gaspara was never a courtesan, because she remained pure and untouched up to the age of twenty-six. From Collaltino, she never accepted anything as the price for her favors, but always accused him of ingratitude and betrayal. Her rapport with Zen was superficial and platonic. And in no reliable document does it appear that she was ever the lover of another man. (69)

Whereas Salza's language is scholarly and a bit moralistic, Cesareo's is emphatic and often sarcastic. Both men sin in the same fashion. Convinced of their own arguments, they construe the data to suit their prejudices.

Other critics were less adamant but more realistic. Taking Stampa's defense were Eugenio Donadoni, G. A. Borgese, Giovanni Rabizzani, Innocenzi Greggio, and Cesareo. It was Donadoni, a highly respected critic, who suggested that the poet had not been a courtesan, nor had she been "a warm virginal soul," but rather one of the century's "irregulars." In a review of Donadoni's monograph and Cesareo's book, Gioacchino Brognoligo offered a reasonable solution to the biographical dilemma, a solution which could explain both the poet's morals and her activities: she was not an amateur but a professional musician, a performer, a true *virtuosa*. This seems a likely if unproven explanation and it accounts for the emphasis her contemporaries placed on her musical accomplishments, her access to salons and patrician houses, her financial situation, dependent on patronage rather than inherited wealth, her emancipation and direct contact with men and women of all stations, and, finally, the ease with which she entered the affair with the Count di Collalto.

These critical polemics and heated literary battles point to an obvious flaw in the approach to Gaspara Stampa: it was the woman and not the poet who enchanted critics and artists alike. Stampa personified a myth, whether it was that of the *appassionata*, the betrayed virgin, the sinner redeemed by love, or the emancipated woman. Even her fall from grace elicited fictional possibilities. One Luigi Pompily followed in Carrer's footsteps, creating another fiction-alized biography of the Renaissance poet; but rather than the abandoned maiden destined for death, which had appealed to the Romantics, Pompily sought to attract a modern audience with a human drama of sin and redemption through love, a Renaissance *Traviata* possessed of all the melodrama, corruption, and despair, if not the immortal music, of the Verdi opera. Titled *Gasparina, the Love Story of an Adventurous and Celebrated Poet,* the book was published in 1936, obtaining a small measure of success. The appeal of a legend, no matter how fallacious, is strong. As recently as May 1978, the Italian women's magazine *Confidenze* rediscovered the

Carrer letters—together with all the accompanying misconceptions and untruths contained therein—and published a simple article, one of a series on Italian women poets, called "Grace and Regret," which presented itself as a factual account of Stampa's life, although it was little more than the summary of Carrer's text. It added another myth to the Stampian collection by formulating a whimsical query and responding to it. What would Gaspara Stampa's position be in today's society? Would she be a politician? the wife of a prominent man? the organizer of a literary prize? The answer, in keeping with the historical tendency to mythicize the poet's life, was that she would naturally be a generous creature of love, doomed to repeated self-destruction because of her poor choices.

Gaspara's detractors had had their say and her avengers had come to the rescue, increasing scholarly data and defying it with emotional apologies and heated repartee. The "eternal *appassionata*" had replaced the démodé Romantic view. But for more than two centuries, it was not Stampa's poetry that had interested the critics but the mysterious woman who had written it. In 1918, Benedetto Croce had come to accept and solidify Salza's conclusions in an article that characterizes another peculiarity of Stampian criticism: it did not distinguish between real and ideal biography. Basing himself on the poetry for lack of documented evidence, Croce made the *Rime* a biographical source, thereby nullifying the distinction between actual life and its transformation into art. Read in this manner, the poems become stages in the unfolding of Stampa's human itinerary, rather than self-contained creative works.

The question of Gaspara's sex is closely allied to this view of the poetry as versified life history. Just as the single poems were not separated from the biographical episodes which may have inspired them, so too the woman was inseparable from the writer. Discussing the poet's Petrarchismo, Croce paid little heed to the debate over her alleged profession, but did remark upon her sex: "She was a woman; and usually women, when they do not ape men, use poetry by subjecting it to their affections, loving their lover or their children more than poetry." The critic added that a woman's practical nature can be discovered in her paucity of theoretical and contemplative powers. Years later, in a more subtle evaluation of the *Rime*, Croce concluded that the poetry was nothing more than an "epistolary," the "diary" of her love for Collaltino.[10] The notion was not original, although the famous philosopher-critic summarized it admirably. In 1920, Donadoni had already discussed the purposive nature of her inspiration: "She was a poet, almost against her will. She wrote for herself and for him: the sonnets were the letters of her epistolary, the brief and ardent pages of her inner diary."[11] This sexual-biographical approach occasionally went to extremes. Salza explicated the submissive tone of Stampa's poetic pleadings by declaring them an unmistakable sign of her moral degradation and social inferiority. No honest woman or aristocrat would stoop to write so pathetically! Giuseppe Toffanin, a respected Renaissance specialist, took it upon himself to alter the sequence of the *Rime*, so that "the true story can stand out." By doing so, he tampered with the original edition's formal structure and emphasized the importance of the love story rather than the artistic achievement.

From these brief indications, it is apparent that a number of critics classified Stampa's poetry in a stereotypical region often assigned to women writers: they are emotional and impulsive; they write only to vent their feelings; they express themselves instinctively, not rationally; they do not possess artistic distance. The commentators continued to insist upon seeing Stampa's *canzoniere* as the repository of a woman's life, indissolubly uniting the artist and the historical individual. It is a romantic view, and it was to the romantic spirit that Gaspara Stampa most appealed. D'Annunzio mentioned her in his Decadent novel *Il Fuoco*, a modern tale of Venetian passion. Another Decadent, G. A. Borgese, wrote of the "modern and romantic soul" of Stampa's *Rime*. Considering her poetry a mid-point between Petrarca's *Canzoniere* and Goethe's *Werther*, Borgese praised its organic realism, ill-suited to the traditional forms imposed upon it, adding: "This woman who was the first to fashion the modern myth of Love and Death with her flesh and blood was known as a *petrarchista*." Even Abdelkader Salza was captivated, for "the poet succeeds in making us forget the courtesan." [12] The woman had indeed created the poetry, and there is much validity in a biographical interpretation of Stampa's works. But the excessive emphasis placed on the historical figure detracted from the artist who was at work polishing, correcting, and perfecting. She

was a woman, but she was also a poet aware of her craft and of her
need to develop a style of her own, one that could express her content
fully.

"You Who Listen to These Melancholy Rhymes . . ."

The insistent reading of Stampa's poetry as a diary or confession
emphasized its psychological contents but ignored its debt to the
surrounding cultural milieu and lessened its ties to a specific historical
moment. No author produces in a vacuum. The seeds for all writing
come from what is known and available to the artist in his own day,
only to be planted in more or less fertile soil. The writer can then
manipulate, alter, copy, renew, or even reject the materials offered
him. Perhaps more than most periods in literary and social history, the
sixteenth century in Italy was culturally homogeneous. Tastes and
ideals did not vary greatly from town to town, salon to court, country
estate to urban *palazzo*. The education offered was similar from place
to place, as were the expectations, demands, and needs of the relatively
small elite which produced and enjoyed culture. The nobility and its
retinue were a cohesive social group sharing a common system of
values which can be condensed into a few key terms: valor, honor,
courtesy, and faith. The definition of these terms is a complex matter,
however, for they are rich in meaning and refer to different qualities
as they are employed in a specific context. For example, honor might
imply inherited prestige, sexual morality, virginity, social recognition,
or personal and family integrity. Valor could refer to either military or
moral courage, as well as prowess, initiative, boldness, and individual
worth. Faith included religious devotion, but also loyalty and rectitude.
The notion of courtesy derived in part from the medieval *cortesia* and
retained some vestiges of its ancestry, for it alluded to chivalry,
nobility, and an adherence to a specified code of behavior. The code
itself had changed, however. The environment was no longer feudal
but urban and cosmopolitan; the knight had been transformed into a
gentleman. Courtesy now suggested politeness, proper bearing, suitable
demeanor, manners, grace, and urbanity. All four terms, as far as the
educated class was considered, were to be given proper and formal
dress. The Cinquecento respected and demanded external refinement
and decorum. Formalities were adhered to with scrupulous diligence.

It would have been difficult for one of Stampa's contemporaries to imagine a courteous peasant or an honorable bricklayer: the terms were in contradiction. The form prevailed over the content. Such social cohesion was partially a result of the use and acceptance of a common tongue which ignored geographic boundaries in favor of cultural affinities. The *questione della lingua*, or debate over which form of the vernacular to employ as the national tongue, was not a frivolous or facetious matter. It was essential to determine a single, functional medium of expression shared by the entire social class which was responsible for the political, economic, and intellectual life of the peninsula. Predominantly urban and relatively mobile, the elite had expanded in numbers and diversified in makeup; new exigencies required a replacement for Latin as the language of the educated. Eventually, the question was resolved in favor of Cardinal Pietro Bembo's proposal that the modern vernacular be modeled after the great masters of the Tuscan Trecento, Francesco Petrarca and Giovanni Boccaccio, but the issue continued to be debated and discussed. The century was fascinated by the very mechanics of language, resulting in the publication of a number of grammar books, linguistic treatises, and literary analyses. It was the fashion in the salons to discuss techniques of diction, rhetorical devices, and grammatical innuendoes. Conversations centering on language, especially if associated with literature, were as integral a part of social gatherings as the singing of madrigals and the telling of stories, as this brief excerpt from Bandello points out:

> After dining and discussing a variety of things, you picked up a book of the sublime poems of Petrarca. Upon reading a few sonnets, everyone began to highly praise the elevated and straightforward style, the beautiful choice and suitable words, as well as their arrangement, and the hidden meanings poets make use of. Then you began to read the beautiful story of Masinissa and Sofonisba in the *Trionfi*, which is so piteous that it almost drew tears from our eyes.[13]

Standards were established for the proper employment of syntax and style; desirable qualities included decorum, harmony, grace, eloquence, and beauty. The Cinquecento revered words and delighted in their correct use, particularly in conversation. Speakers were much praised for their lexical ingenuity and their ability to manipulate language effectively.

Correct use of language was a social grace to be developed not only in conversation but also in writing, particularly in composing poetry. One of the rudiments of a Renaissance education was prosody; students were taught about meter, form, rhyme, and imagery as a matter of course. As a result, poets flourished and multiplied. Such an abundance of good, bad, average, and absolutely horrendous poets had rarely, if ever, been seen in Italian letters. It is said that every household in Venice boasted its own sonneteer. Poetry had a socializing as well as an artistic function in the Renaissance. Poems were written to amuse and to criticize. Encomiums were especially popular; they were read after dinner in honor of the host or hostess or some important guest, at weddings to honor the couple, at academies and *ridotti* to honor each other. Later, many were collected and published in large volumes, in the spirit of a modern *Festschrift*. Poetry was set to music, proffered as gifts, or sent in place of letters. Poets exchanged compositions and circulated them widely in manuscript. Verse was written to cajole patrons, extort money, eulogize, make friends, and mesmerize. And a great deal of poetry was written as a literary exercise, with no clear purpose. Often, the manufacture of poetry was a craft undertaken by artisans rather than an art. Because of this, it was generally not an original or individualized product, but a mass-produced object which reflected the collective taste. There was a marked uniformity of expression, vocabulary, and content in sixteenth-century lyric poetry, rendering much of it repetitive and monotonous.

Gaspara Stampa adhered to the common taste and some of her poems are clearly little more than exercises in versification. This craftsmanship is clearly visible in the sixty-six compositions forming the "Rime Varie," or miscellaneous poems, of the *Rime*, which were divided into two sections: the "Rime d'Amore" and the "Varie." The conventional nature of Stampa's poetry is discernible in these miscellaneous compositions which conform to the prevailing taste. Some of these occasional poems are expressions of social courtesy and gallantry; they are complimentary declarations of the addressee's distinction, worth, beauty, nobility, and so on. Many are directed to friends and acquaintances; others are addressed to current celebrities, including poets, statesmen, clerics, gentlewomen, and royalty. There is a sequence of four sonnets and a canzone eulogizing a recently deceased nun, the "chaste, dear and favored handmaiden of God" (CCCI). There is also a *capitolo* in praise of the monastic life, which is a prolific warehouse of traditional clichés in favor of the joys and serenity of the convent when compared to the trials and tribulations of married life. To these stock poems, Stampa adds a prothalamian for a "happy couple," some verse in honor of the death of a certain "Socrates," possibly Trifone Gabriele, and a "greeting card" sonnet wishing two friends a speedy recovery from an undisclosed illness. One of the more curious poems in this conventional repertoire is another *capitolo*, a long piece addressed to "my Mirtilla"—presumably the same figure who appears in Carrer's fictitious epistolary—written in terza rima. The poem is effusively sentimental in its longing for her distant friend; its tone is reminiscent of certain adolescent attachments bordering on the abnormal, leading critics to consider it one of the poet's first literary attempts.

The most interesting of the "Varie" are the sonnets directed to the literati of her day: Molin, Michiel, Venier, Speroni, and Della Casa. The majority of these works fall into the category of encomiums and courteous praise. But there is also a strong element of literary commentary and artistic exchange. More than elsewhere, it is in these poems that Stampa addresses herself to the issue of being a writer. Quite often the verses are directed to the problem of being a woman writer. The subjects most often mentioned are style, inspiration, and self-expression. The initial image received is one of artistic insecurity. Whereas Gaspara lauds her male counterparts, most of them followers of Cardinal Bembo's poetics, she consistently denigrates her own poetry. She is only a woman unsure of her talents and literary abilities. There are repeated references to her lacks; in one sonnet, Apollo informs her that she needs "other talent, other style, and other polish . . . or a greater source of eloquence" (CCLXXXVIII). This self-humiliation is a constant throughout the entire opus: "the spirit is ready, but the style is tired" (CCXLVIII). This insecurity is heightened when the poet compares herself and her works to the men—and significantly they are all men—she chooses to extol for their literary

gifts. There is a marked tendency not only to admire, which is the
nature of a panegyric, but also to belittle herself in doing so. The
following passage from a sonnet addressed to Girolamo Molin is
typical and exemplifies this inclination:

> Io vorrei ben, Molin (ma non ho l'ale
> da prender tanto e sì gradito volo),
> portar, scrivendo, a l'uno e l'altro polo
> l'alta cagion del mio foco immortale;
>   ché l'opra e la materia è tanta e tale,
> ed io son sì dal mal vinta e dal duolo,
> che a ciò non basto, e voi bastate solo,
> od altrui stile al vostro stile eguale. (CCLX)

(I would indeed wish, Molin [but have not the wings for such great
and pleasant flight], to carry the noble cause of my immortal flame far
and wide in my writing, but the task and matter are so great and such,
and I am so overcome by woe and grief, that I do not suffice; only you
suffice, or perhaps another whose style is equal to your own.)

In these poetic comparisons, the key word employed by Stampa is
always *stile,* often accompanied by *volo* and *opra.* The lexical choice is
suggestive. It implies that the poet has well-defined ideas on the nature
of the creative act and set standards with which to compare herself
and her poetry. *Stile* can be broadly translated as "style" but in usage
it also suggests talent, ability, know-how, the creative process, and, as
noted by Maria Bellonci, revealed poetry. *Opra* has both the meaning
of a completed work, the entire *opus,* and the activity of writing
necessary to produce the work. Joined with *volo*—flight, ascent,
imagination, the means of obtaining height—the terms present, or at
least infer, Stampa's approach to her own literary production: it is an
active search, the difficult task of harnessing one's talents in order to
achieve artistic heights. It is not a spontaneous outburst but a planned,
considered, and conscious attempt to obtain poetic self-expression.

It appears that Stampa had a personal, preestablished ideal to which
she aspired but could not reach, for "my style does not answer to my
desire" (CCXLIX). It is this stylistic achievement she praises in
others. Venier is admired for "such great style, such ready rhymes"

(CCLII), Speroni for his "famous and honored works" (CCLIII), and Molin for his "learned and honored rhymes" (CCLXI). In their abilities, she sees her own deficiencies, but there is also the desire to achieve and a goal to accomplish. Stampa explains her failure to obtain the sought-after *stile* as correlative to her being a woman, rather than a man, equating her sex with artistic weakness. While men follow the path of knowledge and science she, "a woman and humble," cannot follow, for her "lowliness would offend such labor" (CCLI). Clearly, sexual frailty is synonymous with intellectual weakness, influencing her power to create. Her sex is made responsible for her inability to take flight, to accomplish adequate self-expression. It is the artisan, not the art, which is disparaged.

As the source of her own inspiration Stampa cites Amor, love, which appears in the *Rime* both as an abstract idea and in personified form. Love as the inspiration of art is an old literary *topos* which dates back to the origins of Italian literature. True to this tradition, Gaspara introduces herself as the servant of love, crediting Amor's inspiration and not her own abilities for the success of her poetic endeavors. Often Amore is incarnated in the person of the beloved, who then becomes the source of her art. Thus, the issue of writing is inseparable from that of loving. In the "Rime d'Amore," Stampa stresses this indivisibility, while continuing to emphasize her own nullification in the process. Love, or the beloved, is presented as the moving force behind her works:

> . . . .
> voi movete lo stil, l'arte, l'ingegno,
> sensi, spirti, pensier, voglie, alma e core.
>   Se da me dunque nasce cosa buona,
>   è vostra, non è mia: voi mi guidate,
>   a voi si deve il pregio e la corona.
>   Voi, non me, da qui indietro omai lodate
>   di quanto per me s'opra e si ragiona;
>   ché l'ingegno e lo stil, signor, mi date. (CLVII)

(. . . you move my style, art, talent, senses, spirits, thoughts, desire, soul, and heart. Thus, if any good is born of me, it's yours, not mine; you guide me, the merit and wreath are justly yours. Praise

yourself, not me, for all that is done or said through me, because,
Sir, you give me both talent and style.)

Thus, whereas Stampa belittles herself on an artistic level in the
miscellaneous poems addressed to her friends and mentors, she
magnifies Amor or the beloved by lessening herself in the love poetry.
There is, however, an innate contradiction at work within the *Rime*.
While recognizing the apparent inspiration of an external force, which
she associates with either Love or the beloved, the poet is also
cognizant of the power of art and, thereby, of her own power as the
wielder of words.

This knowledge is first presented in the dedication to Collaltino di
Collalto. In that letter, she makes a case for the strength of words,
their ability to speak for themselves without intermediaries: "Why am
I . . . insulting even my rhymes, as though they were unable to present
themselves and needed someone else's help?" Stampa is indirectly
declaring the independent nature of the artistic creation, which is not
indivisibly tied to either the author or the historical moment but is
self-sufficient and self-contained. She is also implying that her art is
successful for it expresses her intentions without further need of
explanations. The poetry stands alone for it is art.

Stampa's *Rime* have ceaselessly been read as a historical document,
functioning as a source upon which critics have fashioned her life
story. The poetry cannot reasonably be interpreted as a factual text,
however. If it is biographical, it deals with spiritual and psychological
biography. Emotional states may be honestly rendered, but they have
been adjusted to the constraints of a literary form, generally the
sonnet. Such alterations and the very act of recreating factual moments
to suit artistic demands require a shift in perspective. The points of
view of the poet and of the person are necessarily different and often
at variance. In the past, Gaspara Stampa was simply considered a
woman in love who wrote about it. As Donadoni stated: "The poems
are . . . an outlet for passion; they are life; they are poetry; they rarely
become art: or, perhaps, the one great art of the poet is that she does
not make art. . . . Her book is primarily the document of a throbbing
woman's heart, more than a poetic fiction." More emotionally, Ada
Negri, a celebrated author herself, exclaimed: "Woman, woman,

woman, in love and stupid, on her knees and giving way in the unequal battle of love; but she was able to give living shape to her own human misery in the most perfect artistic sincerity ever achieved by any feminine creature in this world."[14] The woman continued to dominate the artist; the poetry remained subservient to the legend. But art must stand or fall on its own merits. Gaspara Stampa needs to be studied not as a woman who also wrote, but as a poet who described, presented, and quite possibly invented situations, rendering life fiction in order to elevate it to true art.

Life infuses art and art contains life; successful poetry is the ideal fusion of the two. Although she had never formulated her own poetics or made statements on aesthetics, Stampa was aware of this symbiosis. She was also conscious of the insufficiency of art to totally capture and express life. But this did not prevent her from making the attempt a hundred times over. Her search for a personal *stile* never slackened, for she knew that good poetry required revision, reworking, time, and effort, as well as talent. The admiration she bestowed on her contemporaries was essentially in recognition of their literary skills; they were able to shape language and forge their own styles. They had achieved the personal diction that she sought for herself. While the critics charged her with writing for immediate, personal ends, such as communicating with her beloved, obtaining his interest, and renewing his affection, the poetry itself belies this assertion. Stampa recognized the power of poetry and, consequently, the power of the writer to grant enduring life in the timeless world of art. Poetry provided immortality for the creative work, its protagonists, and the creator. This immunity from the ravages of death and history were hers to give: ". . . I will see if, by using the virtue granted me, my pages can make you famous for future centuries" (**CXXXVIII**). Thus, Stampa declares her own power to give eternal fame, a fame which extends also to herself, in the present as well as the future. There is an undercurrent of pride beneath Gaspara's protestations of submissive inferiority. She is proud of her capacity for loving, her exceptional devotion, and remarkable fidelity. But she is also proud of her poetic vein. While she may claim Love's inspiration, or Collaltino's, it is really her own talents and ambition that produced the *Rime*. "It is precisely the artist, and not the perfect image, who inspires herself, creating this new style and this immortality."[15] Through her writing, she achieved personal assertion and individual recognition, possibly denied her in life: "So I turn to write only the story of my happy pangs, that make me singular among people" (CXIV). It is loving which makes her unique, but it is the writing alone which makes possible recognition. Without the material act, her singularity cannot be known; the greatness of her passion is dependent upon her verbalization of it. Therefore, the quest for an adequate *stile* was also the pursuit of individual fulfillment as a woman and as an artist. Being a child of the sixteenth century, she sought to adapt herself to its standards of aesthetic beauty. The Renaissance demanded structure and form in its art; Stampa attempted to give her poetry such shape.

The Text

The text of the *Rime* which is generally employed today is Abdelkader Salza's 1913 edition, in which he published both the poetry of Gaspara Stampa and that of Veronica Franco. This particular edition was based on the 1554 original, edited by Cassandra Stampa and Giorgio Benzone on the poet's autograph, which was either lost or destroyed. It can only be presumed that the first edition was organized in accordance with the author's desires and in keeping with the skeleton of the work as presented by the lost manuscript. It is a rigorously structured text, separated into thematic and formal divisions. The major groupings are the "Rime d'Amore" and the "Rime Varie." The subdivisions are purely technical: the madrigals and *capitoli* are placed after the rest of the poetry, forming categories of their own. When preparing his edition, Salza made some major alterations in the sequence of the original. He separated the text into two categories— love poetry and miscellaneous works—to a greater extent than did the 1554 *Rime* and, to achieve this goal, he placed the madrigals and *capitoli* which did not relate to the love story into the category of "Varie." The miscellaneous compositions were then reordered so that thematic groupings could be arranged; for example, the poems written to eulogize the dead nun, previously scattered, were united. The sequence of the sonnets written for Bartolomeo Zen was altered and, finally, the poems of religious contrition were removed from the "Rime d'Amore" and placed at the end of the book.[16] To recapitulate, modern editions, based on Salza's work, are divided into two large sections. The love poems, numbering more than two hundred sonnets, two sestinas, and a canzone, follow more or less chronologically the developments of the love for Collaltino and, later, Zen. These are immediately followed by nineteen madrigals and, separately, the five *capitoli* that deal with the love story. The "Rime Varie" include all the occasional poetry addressed to her friends, acquaintances, and a few celebrities; most of these works are sonnets, but there are also a few *capitoli* and a canzone. The final section which concludes the *canzoniere* is made up of eight sonnets of religious contrition. In all there are 311 poems comprising the *Rime*. Salza's edition also returned to the orthography and punctuation of the original, which had been altered by previous editors, all too eager to modernize syntax and vocabulary in order to make it a more readable text for modern audiences, at the expense of authenticity.

Sonnets dominate Stampa's *Rime,* followed at a distance by the madrigals. The love poetry composes more than two-thirds of the text, some 253 works, including the sonnets of contrition. References to her great love for Collaltino are also to be found in the "Varie," generally in connection with her stylistic inabilities to capture it, or him, on paper. It is not surprising that Croce chose to define the *Rime* as "nothing more than the epistolary or diary of her principal and great love." Editors and commentators chose to view the text in this manner as well. Great dissatisfaction was expressed at the work's rigorous divisions; a more accurate recording of Gaspara's passion for her count was considered especially desirable. An oft-heard proposal was the integration of the madrigals and *capitoli* into the fabric of the love poems. Some ambitious souls went so far as to carry out the modifications so that the plot line would stand out more clearly. In her study *Gaspara Stampa*, published in 1893, Elissa Minozzi suggested an alternative distribution of the poems so that the readers could better follow the story. In 1929, Toffanin made the transfer of thought into deed and reordered part of the *Rime* for his anthology *Le più belle pagine di Gaspara Stampa, Vittoria Colonna, Veronica Gambara, Isabella di Morra;* his purpose, like Minozzi's, was to strengthen the love story, by making it more logical and cohesive.

But the formal structure is an integral part of the *Rime*. While it may appear contrived to those wishing to read a story through the poetry, it is a sign of Stampa's interest, if not expertise, in the stylistic and organizational aspects of writing. Cassandra's dedication had clearly stated that the poetry had been produced "partially to exercise her talents," namely as a literary exertion. The very existence of the miscellaneous verse confirms this. Although not devoid of social meaning, the "Varie" are certainly not the results of a direct amatory stimulus or inspiration. They are exercises in the art of writing; their inspiration is purely stylistic and literary. Nor should this be surprising given the nature of her friendships and the caliber of her life and interests. Composition interested and fascinated her, as it did her peers. It is significant that the first edition of the *Rime* was dedicated to Giovanni Della Casa, one of the most stylistically innovative poets of the Renaissance, for whom—if Cassandra's letter is to be believed— Gaspara expressed great respect, "praising your very learned, very graceful, and very serious compositions to the skies, as the rivals of any of the ancients or moderns that are read." It is also significant that Francesco Sansovino would dedicate a rather theoretical work to her, the publication of Benedetto Varchi's lesson on a sonnet by Della Casa, adding that "your worth and your purified judgment far exceed any common praise."

The very organization of the *Rime* indicated the presence of an artist at work, chiseling, polishing, and perfecting her creation. Unfortunately, no known variants exist for Stampa's poetry, so it is impossible to make comparisons between an initial and a final draft of the same composition in order to demonstrate corrections and reworkings. The fact, however, that the poet died a full three years after the conclusion of her affair with Collaltino but continued working on her *canzoniere*, as indicated in Cassandra's letter, suggests that Stampa did indeed revise her poems. It is apparent that the so-called diary underwent organizational remodeling as well, for it is unfeasible to conclude that the madrigals were composed after the sonnets or that the miscellaneous verse chronologically followed the love sonnets. No positive dating is available for the works, although it is possible to make educated guesses as to their time of composition. Thematically, the first poems of the *Rime* serve as an introduction to the text, suggesting that they were placed there purposely, at a time posterior to composition. In Petrarchan fashion, a prefatory sonnet addressed to the readers presents the various themes and sets the tone for the volume:

> Voi, ch'ascoltate in queste meste rime,
> in questi mesti, in questi oscuri accenti
> il suon degli amorosi miei lamenti
> e de le pene mie tra l'altre prime,
>   ove fia chi valor apprezzi e stime,
> gloria, non che perdon, de' miei lamenti
> spero trovar fra le ben nate genti,
> poi che la lor cagione è sì sublime. (I)

(I hope to find you among the well-born folk, you who listen to the sound of my amorous complaints and to my grief, which is greater than any other's, as told in these melancholy rhymes, in these melancholy and obscure accents. Wherever valor is appreciated and esteemed, I hope to find glory as well as pardon for my complaints since their cause is so sublime.)

The restructuring of her *canzoniere* and the allusion to a public suggest that Stampa obviously intended to publish, or at least circulate, her poetry.

When compared to the majority of *canzonieri*, however, Stampa's *Rime* differ in both style and content. A distinguishing feature of this poetry is its language, which is far more immediate and spontaneous than that of most academic verse. Its tone has been called prosaic, which has accentuated the general inclination to read it not as art but as a confession or epistolary in verse. Like all other such works, Stampa's *canzoniere* is essentially a love story whose transfigured reality is contemplated in its varying stages and moments. Unlike many other *canzonieri*, however, the *Rime* are closely tied to precise events, individuals, and occasions in the poet's biography. The "Rime d'Amore" relate episodes occupying a four-year period: an early happy time of requited love for Count Collaltino di Collalto, tarnished only by a bit of chilliness on his part; he sings and she admires his sweet voice; he leaves for his estates, she suffers; they meet again but he announces his imminent departure for France; in his absence she writes, weeps, remains faithful; he sends word of his return and she experiences a renewed feeling of joy while preparing to welcome him; they spend a beatific night together; her joy is mingled with jealousy; he leaves again, they reunite; she joins him on his fief; he torments her with his demands, accusations, and threats of abandonment; more separations and more pain; his last departure; a period of meditation is followed by the appearance of a new love on the horizon; she hesitates; her new happiness is mingled with the memories of her past suffering; she yields to her heart, accepting her destiny of eternal *appassionata*. As a biography, the *Rime* offer only schematic details at best. The book's greatest value lies in the poet's rich description of her changing psychological states. Nuances of emotion are subtly expressed; explosions of feeling are boldly stated. Stampa the *persona* is alternately passionate and submissive, plaintive and victorious, bold and humble, desolate and fulfilled, nostalgic and demanding. Love's eternal tale is told in its multiplicity of faces, embodied in one woman, one lover. At its best, Gaspara Stampa's poetry expresses a universal condition: the moments, emotions, aspirations, and sufferings of those who love greatly and exclusively. And showing her the way, Stampa had one great master: Francesco Petrarca.

Chapter Three

Masters and Disciples: A School for Poetry

The Confines of Imitation

The *Canzoniere* of Francesco Petrarca was the stimulus behind most lyric poetry produced in Renaissance Italy. Written in the fourteenth century, the work had astonishing import for well over three centuries and received vast diffusion throughout Europe. It embodied the literary and moral ideals of an age—the sixteenth century—fulfilling its intellectual needs and offering an acceptable approach to its poetic expectations. The choice of Petrarca's poetry as the model for entire generations of versifiers was prompted by specific exigencies found in the Renaissance mentality. The very selection of a model implied the search for one and the demand for it. Such a desire had its historical origins in Humanism and the rediscovery of Italy's classical heritage. Renaissance literally means rebirth and the men of the early Renaissance believed that the return to the past could elevate the present; they saw themselves as renovators, not originators. Great respect was paid the Greco-Roman heritage of Italy, a respect which surpassed any given to more recent thought. In the fifteenth century, Humanists had rediscovered, reread, reevaluated, and recirculated the ancient texts. It was an incredible explosion of old ideas suddenly become new.

Early Humanism was characterized by the discovery and gathering of classical books, which were then edited and later translated. Erudites constituted the nucleus devoted to such studies. Scholarship was conducted in Latin and Greek rather than in the vernacular. But the introduction of the printing press to Italy toward the end of the fifteenth century considerably altered the situation. With the advent of print, books became relatively cheap to purchase, compared to the expensive and difficult to obtain manuscripts that were written by hand. At first, considerable attention was paid to the classics. In

Venice, Aldus Manutius and his circle devoted themselves to the diffusion of the ancients; they spent considerable time in philological studies and the reconstruction of texts so that the printed book would be not only interesting, but also accurate. The Greek revival in printing was centered in Venice toward the turn of the century, but Aldus's sons continued their father's inspired work after his death through most of the sixteenth century. For the Aldine press, the diffusion of classical texts was a labor of love, rooted in the Humanist traditions of the early Renaissance.

Another consequence of printing was the creation of an ever-larger public to read the books. It was a classic example of the snowball effect: the more books that were made available, the more people read. After its initial concentration on Greco-Roman works, the printing press churned out a variety of matter: books on history and geography, texts on anatomy, scientific treatises, biographies, commercial manuals, and literary works. One major issue was still unresolved: the choice of language. Whereas Latin was the tongue of erudition and scholarship, it was not the language of the masses, nor was it readily understood by merchants, women, bureaucrats, and many an aristocrat, whose passing knowledge of the august tongue was adequate but hardly fluent. If reading was to become a pleasure and an accessible source of information, rather than an academic chore, it needed to be presented in the spoken language of the people. The question raised, however, was: which language? The choice was difficult because the selection was vast. There were the major dialects, such as Venetian and Florentine, courtly Italian—but which court? Rome? Ferrara? Urbino?—and the speech of the merchant class. The problem was aggravated by the number of existing dialects which changed not only from city to city but also from class to class. It was also complicated by the fact that Tuscan had become a valid literary language used in both poetry and prose for over two hundred years. It was not an idle issue. Books were becoming of paramount value for human communications, shipping, commerce, science, government, international affairs, and education. A standardized tongue was not only desirable but imperative. A solution was sought and eventually found. The man to credit was a Venetian patrician: Pietro Bembo.[1]

Bembo dictated the literary tastes of the sixteenth century. Rarely has one man exerted such influence on the culture of a society, nor has one man often encompassed so totally the needs, tastes, aspirations, and mentality of an age. In the Quattrocento the admiration for antiquity had allowed Italian intellectuals to create a literary tradition founded not in the present but in the past. The use of Latin provided a continuum with this legacy, while also symbolizing a rejection of the unacceptable aspects of the Middle Ages. But as the vernacular asserted itself ever more strongly, it began supplanting the Humanist tradition. The oft-debated *questione della lingua,* which occupied the minds and filled the pages of Renaissance intellectuals, was not mere academic bicker but the Renaissance battleground in the war between the ancients and the moderns. It was a struggle between tradition and novelty, quiescence and change. In it the external, fixed beauty of the classics encountered the fluid mutability of the spoken word. There were those who favored the retention of Latin as the literary tongue, but the discussions were moving perceptibly toward the vernacular. The Italian language was coming into its own. Bembo's work, the *Prose della volgar lingua,* synthesized the various points of views operative in the debate and offered a solution which did not please everyone but satisfied many.

Although the text was drafted years earlier, Bembo published the *Prose* in 1525; the contents were already common knowledge among many scholars and cultured people, for the manuscript had been widely circulated. Like many Renaissance treatises, the work was in dialogue form, depicting a serious but friendly discussion between educated men. Among the interlocutors, Bembo placed various individuals who could typify the diverse approaches to the issue. Ercole Strozzi argued on behalf of pure Latin Humanism, whereas the pragmatic Giuliano de' Medici defended the vernacular, meaning of course everyday speech, which he considered lively because of its constant state of flux. Bembo's brother, Carlo, was chosen to be Pietro's spokesman. Carlo urged the creation of a superior tongue forged not on current speech but derived from the application of classical standards to the vernacular. A classicist himself, Bembo was attracted to the unalterable elegance of Latin, which had a quality of linguistic perfection because of its fixity. The same had to be achieved for the Italian: it had to be fixed, classicized. Bembo's solution included the adoption of specific models who represented stylistic excellence and beauty.[2] The choice fell on Francesco Petrarca, especially as the author of graceful, clear, and refined verse, and on Giovanni Boccaccio, writer of the *Decameron,* for his polished prose, which resembled in its syntax and arrangement the flow of Ciceronian Latin.

Bembo's linguistic theories sought to standardize the vernacular through the imitation of models. A similar attempt at linguistic stability was being undertaken by grammarians who sought to establish rules for a fundamentally unstructured language. The two principal texts were both products of Venetian scholarship: Fortunio's *Regole della volgar lingua* (1516) and Liburnio's *Vulgari elegantiae* (1521), both published before Pietro Bembo's *Prose.* Of the three works, Bembo's text was doubtlessly the most influential. Its positing of a Tuscan norm, based on the great writers of the Trecento, found a receptive audience, for it satisfied the need for an acceptable literary Italian while also paying homage to the Humanist tradition. Bembo had never negated the value of the classics—he was himself a versatile and elegant Latinist—but he had recognized the inevitable growth and eventual supremacy of the vernacular. Rather than reject it, as many of his erudite companions did, Bembo chose to take the *volgare* into the classical fold. A conciliation between modern needs and ancient prerogatives was found by rendering the vernacular as immutable as possible. The selection of literary authorities and their enthronement as the rulers of language permitted the establishment of a classical Italian that was invulnerable to the attacks of time and fashion. Bembo's notions became quickly popular and the *Prose della volgar lingua* was unquestionably a literary milestone and a seminal work, if judged only on the basis of the twenty-six editions it underwent in the sixteenth century alone.

Literary Italian was to be based on the imitation of the works of the great writers of the fourteenth century: Dante in part, Boccaccio, and most of all Petrarca. The second book of the *Prose* attacked the issue of "the manner in which one writes" by analyzing the qualities found in these exemplary authors, judging them on the bases of invention, choice of vocabulary, purity, sweetness, harmony, solemnity, order, and gracefulness. The third book discussed grammatical issues, such as the use of nouns, adjectives, prepositions, verbs, and so on. As can be seen, the *Prose* form a total corpus on the subject of language: theoretic, idealistic, and practical. While the grammatical treatises had dealt only with how a language was employed, Bembo provided an aesthetic ideal to follow. In short, he latinized Italian for his contemporaries, rendering it harmonic, orderly, fixed, elegant, and invariable. While giving coherence to the vernacular, he also resolved important problems of style which preoccupied his age. "The Renaissance aspired to style, intensely examined classical precedents, and strove to imitate their measure, elegance and order as faithfully as possible."[3]

The choice of models proposed by Bembo was consonant with the Renaissance's respect for, and emulation of, the classics. It was the quest for an ideal in a society devoted to the establishment of paragons. The Cinquecento demonstrated a strong predilection for form, considering it an extension of harmony and decorum. Poetry was rigorously metered and structured according to the traditional patterns of sonnets, canzone, madrigals, ottava rima, ballads, and so forth. Plays were required to follow the Aristotelean unities. Precedents were honored. Bembo merely expressed the inherent tendencies of his era. For the Renaissance, the presence of a model was an aid, not a handicap. Imitation was not considered a hindrance or a barrier to creativity. Indeed, it is only within the confines of imitation that the lyric poetry of the Cinquecento, including Gaspara Stampa's own works, can be fully understood and appreciated.

For the sixteenth century, imitation represented a highly prized manner of writing.[4] Throughout the Middle Ages and Humanism, the ancients had been looked to for guidance, ideas, and inspiration. The classics were approached with understanding and empathy; their taste, manners, and ideals were assimilated into the culture of the Renaissance, not merely studied. Imitation was the norm, but it was not conceived as the mere rewriting or remaking of the model. Originality was not excluded, but it was limited by the existence of a prototype. The language, form, and thought of the traditional standard was to be emulated, not copied. By being reworked, the original was necessarily altered and renewed, producing an imitation which could be unique and beautiful, even novel, if in a subtle manner. Newness was not expected or greatly admired; creative embroidery was.

Although the existence of a model was generally favored, some scholars, notably G. Francesco Pico, preferred having a variety of prototypes from which to choose. Pico called these *i migliori*, "the best." Bembo rejected this notion, opting for his own concept of *l'ottimo*, "the very best." Bembo felt that only one major standard was possible; two perfections could not exist. He was also disturbed by the necessarily hybrid and eclectic nature of a work which imitated a number of sources. "Bembo's position was that the concept of style was not innate, but was developed as a result of observing other writers and that a consistent style could only be achieved by following a sole model of excellence, not by eclecticism; ultimately the model could be transcended."[5] The desire for perfection in style required not disparate examples, but a single ideal. And ideals tend to be unitary, not dispersive. To develop an individual style, each poet required a specific role model on which to form himself. Eclecticism implied comparison and contrast of models and, thereby, uncertainty and a lack of purity.

The ideal prototype contained not only the style of the single author but the summation of the entire literary tradition which had gone into forming him. Thus, Petrarca represented not only himself, but—through him—the entire classical world he had assimilated, as well as the Provençal poets, the Dolce Stil Nuovo, the Sicilian school, and the troubadouric tradition. He assembled and integrated all of these into his own poetry, becoming the depository of literary tradition. The encounter of the model and the imitator was the meeting of the present with the choice elements of the cultural past. In the best of cases, the product of this encounter integrated tradition and surpassed it. Thus, the rivalry between the Renaissance artist and the standard did not destroy creativity but aided it, as long as one accepted the limits within which the literature of imitation operated.

Imitation was not seen as the crystallization of art by the majority of poets and writers producing in the Renaissance, but as an active interchange between emulated and emulator. On the whole, imitation was preponderantly directed at style rather than content. A poet was considered successful on the grounds of his ability to give beautiful, ideal dress to the most humble of contents. Excellence lay in the ability to rise above everyday reality and enter a realm where decorum, grace, elegance, and aesthetics reigned. Verisimilitude was praised, and naturalism was not, for poetry had to exist outside the quotidian. The model offered infinite possibilities of variations for the modern poet. Imitation was an active search for new ways of dealing with similar subjects and similar forms while operating a slight modification and hinting at a new perspective, an original inspiration, or a different literary source. It was very much like a card game, where each card is given a distinct value, the rules set, and the goal established, yet no one game is identical to another, for each player-poet must play his own hand. Because imitation had become a dogma of criticism, poetry had changed into a rational exercise for many writers in the sixteenth century. To be classical was to be reasonable, clear, decorous, and harmonious; this did not include subjectivity, individuality, or experimentation. As far as poetry was concerned, the Renaissance favored authority, the status quo, and the known rather than the flight of fancy, innovation, or rebellion. Any innovation took place within the established structures. The new poet was to compete with the old model by following the rules of the game and using the same deck of cards.

Francesco Petrarca's Influence

It was inevitable that Bembo's choice of a model for poetry fall on Francesco Petrarca for the works of the great master of the fourteenth century were clearly in harmony with the taste of the Cinquecento. Petrarca's polished verse, clarity, grace, structured form, and aestheticism appealed to the period's aspirations to *buon gusto,* refinement, and style. The poet's *Canzoniere* seemed to embody the artistic values of the Renaissance: harmony, which consisted in the quantity, quality, and position of sounds and words, a term closely allied to proportion and order, which implied formal structures; grace, which referred rather broadly to sweetness, elegance, and a pleasing *je ne sais quoi;* an aesthetic sense of opulence or richness, including variety, grandeur, abundance, and splendor, as well as magnificence, greatness, sumptuousness, and dignity. The five major concepts in literary criticism were decorum, grandeur, grace, variety, and similitude. "In literature, decorum involved the crucial problem of suiting the form *(forma)* to the content *(materia).*"[6] Because of its express nature as a spiritual attachment, Petrarca's love for Laura—lapses into sensuality notwithstanding—complemented the flowering of Neo-Platonism and the popularity of treatises on love, while the poet's inner contradictions and restlessness echoed the uncertainty and instability of Renaissance life. Petrarca was looked upon as the perfect lover expressing the perfect love in an imperfect world. But he had also been conscious of the frailty of human life and had felt the pull of religion and repentence. "In this precise cultural moment, Petrarca was proposed to poetic taste as he who had truly loved and endured passions in his very depths; he was the modern man, the poet overflowing with his classical past, and steeped, to the point of Augustinian piety, in an elect type of Christianity."[7] It is not that the age suited itself to Petrarca, but that Petrarca was admirably suited for the Renaissance.

Petrarchismo, the imitation and emulation of the poet's works, was the answer to a collective need and the expression of a collective spirit. Petrarca proved exemplary on two levels, unlike Boccaccio: the aesthetic and the moral. Not only were his syntax, vocabulary, images, and themes imitated, but he also became a *specchio di vita*,[8] a model of life and behavior, a mirror in which the Renaissance lover could see himself reflected in all the psychological and emotional complexities of love, and in which the modern sinner could see the path of temptation rejected in favor of mournful contrition and pleas to heaven. His was the ideal *iter*, elevated to the symbolic level of myth. Petrarca was an archetype in which each reader and imitator could find a part of themselves. Petrarchan imitation offered its adherents two clearly defined characteristics. On the one hand, there was the reality of a human experience of love, suffering, moral struggle, spiritual fatigue, frustration, degradation, and longing, a reflection of the darker currents in Renaissance life. On the other, the *Canzoniere*'s aesthetic perfection presented an absolute to counter and offset the temporal and the uncertain elements of life. Through art, it was possible to harmonize those passions which could not be balanced by men in their daily existence. Art promised control, form, and beauty, whereas life begrudgingly tendered only brief glimpses of such treasures. The inherent contradiction in Renaissance life lay beneath its fascination with style and models; beauty and decorum covered delusion, converting it and overcoming it by elevating it to the higher sphere of art. Life was filtered, and thus made palatable, through the words and experiences of one man, whose private literary lexicon became the universal vocabulary for generations of lyric poets. To depict the world in poetry in the sixteenth century was to depict it in the language of Francesco Petrarca.

The critical commentaries produced in the Cinquecento concerned themselves with the two major aspects of Petrarchismo: the stylistic and the moral. There were numerous works devoted to textual exegesis. These were often technical critiques occupied with the issues of form and language. Imitators could learn the methods of achieving correct expression and develop acceptable if mediocre poetic skills by studying such texts. Rhyming dictionaries were also published, as were lexicons of Petrarchan terminology and studies on morphology. Stylistically and linguistically, the *Canzoniere* was so widely accepted as the poetic standard that the vocabulary of sixteenth century lyric poetry derived not from contemporary usage but directly from Petrarca's verse. Words, phrases, even entire lines were "borrowed" by the poet's eager emulators without fear of censure. Indeed, such borrowings were expected and constitute a major feature of Renaissance poetry. The incredible emphasis placed on language and style is perhaps the major reason for the multitude of insignificant versifiers who fed on the model like parasites without contributing any fresh insights or creative energy of their own.

Petrarca the model lover, spiritual guide, contrite sinner, and restless seeker of inner peace also provided critics with ample room for commentaries. At times, the *Canzoniere* was interpreted as a narrative biography or as a historical document. Alessandro Vellutello's 1528 edition of the work boasted a map of the area surrounding Avignon, where many of the love poems are situated, so that the reader might familiarize himself with the locale's geography.

Bembo's interest in the works of Petrarca did not stop with his statements in the *Prose della volgar lingua,* which literally crowned the *trecentista* the sole authority on poetry. Working for Aldus Manutius, Pietro Bembo prepared the principal edition of Petrarca's *Canzoniere* in 1501 by working with the finest extant manuscript from the fourteenth century. The work was so philologically correct that it served as the source for all subsequent editions in the Cinquecento. But Bembo's own *Rime,* first issued in 1530, are equally important. Next to Petrarca's, this was the most popular *canzoniere* of the century, undergoing some thirty printings in less than a hundred years. These *Rime* are also significant because they are material examples of Bembo's theories on imitation put into practice. While rarely read today, Bembo's poetry was highly acclaimed by his peers and contemporaries. Lodovico Dolce declared Pietro second only to Petrarca and this view was widely shared. Bembismo, a natural offshoot of its parent Petrarchismo, was the imitation of Cardinal Pietro's works, rather than the master's, so that a *bembista* was basically a third generation *petrarchista* and a second generation imitator.

The list of known *petrarchisti* and *bembisti* is exceptionally long and rather tedious. Let it suffice that every major household produced one or more rhymesters. Venice was a major incubator for writers of all types. The first professional authors, called *poligrafi*, worked in the city and it was the meeting place of the *bembisti*. Most books of poetry were also published there. Between 1540 and 1560, the years of Gaspara Stampa's maturity, one publishing house, Giolito, issued Petrarca's *Canzoniere* twenty-two times. Boccaccio's *Decameron* received only nine printings. An obvious monitor of the period's taste! The majority of new contemporary poets were also first published by Venetian editors. Anthologies of poetry, such as the one in which three of Stampa's sonnets appeared, were produced fairly regularly. Almost all the critical commentaries on Petrarca were brought out in the laguna city, including the early work by Filelfo and the later, important texts by Castelvetro.

Since Venice was one of the Italian centers of literary activity, it is not surprising that Gaspara Stampa would have more than a passing acquaintance with the issues and figures involved. Many of her friends and acquaintances were avowed *bembisti:* Trifone Gabriele had been an intimate and a literary associate of Pietro Bembo; Domenico Venier's circle was predominantly composed of literati who espoused the Cardinal's theories and considered versifying a serious task; Torquato Bembo, Pietro's son, was a friend. Others, like Speroni and Della Casa, were actively involved in the *questione della lingua*, as well as being dedicated scholars. Even had Gaspara not been associated with the intellectual groups of her city, she would have inevitably known Petrarca's works, and known them well. His presence in the cultural world of the Renaissance was not only visible but pervasive. Everyone read Francesco Petrarca, most admired him, some mocked, and quite a few imitated. Young girls were allowed to read the *Canzoniere* alongside their inspirational books; priests utilized his celebrated life of religious conflict and aspiration to godliness as the subject of their sermons; thousands upon thousands of imitative poems were produced, published, and circulated; no other poet was set to music more often, by Stampa herself for that matter; people sat for their portraits holding a copy of his works; he was cited by all as one of the major authorities on love; the *Canzoniere* was the Renaissance best-seller for decades.

Francesco Petrarca was more than a fashion, infinitely more than a literary fad. His artistic world had been woven into the very fabric of cultural life, concurrently mirroring it, synthesizing it, and typifying its ideals. The *Canzoniere* offered its admirers conflict and chaos, love of woman and love of God, material and physical aspirations alternating with spiritual goals, all presented in a magnificent aesthetic frame. The Renaissance did not formulate a lyric theory, save the imitation of Petrarca. His *Canzoniere* was the epitome of a literary love story, the artistic summit to be conquered, and the perfect *iter* to be followed. And dozens of minor *canzonieri* emulated the great masterwork in all its phases. The consecrated language of love was Petrarca's; his poetry furnished techniques, meters, situations, plots, images, metaphors, and rhyme schemes. The Cinquecento identified with the poetry of Francesco Petrarca. Many of his imitators were poor copies but others, like Gaspara Stampa, followed the master but also presented new options, novel variations on his themes, a slightly different *iter,* a personal voice. Yet, like her contemporaries, Gaspara Stampa was, or at least sought to be, the fervent admirer and dedicated disciple of the great teacher.

Variations on a Poet

Stampa's borrowings from Petrarca are thematic, organizational, syntactic, and technical. Like the master, she depicts a love story as it unfolds in a series of inner conflicts and with painful self-awareness against a backdrop of deceptive dreams and betrayed hopes. Unlike the *Canzoniere,* Gaspara's *Rime* do not involve the death of the beloved, but a similar function is enacted by the poetry of separation; both artists add a number of poems of contrition, which are pleas to God the Father, Christ, or Mary for celestial help and forgiveness. Whereas Stampa orders her miscellaneous verse into a special category, the "Rime Varie," Petrarca's is interspersed in the body of his text. Both poets show an obvious predilection for the sonnet form, but also composed madrigals, sestinas, and canzoni. The loose threads of the plot line are presented in chronological fashion, but in both cases the biographical reality has been filtered through the artistic experience. Living out a love on paper enriched the poet and allowed him to be in control of his feelings by rationalizing them in the labor of harnessing emotion to suit the strictures of poetry.

The opening sonnet of the *Rime* is a tributary paraphrase of the model's prefatory lyric. The imitation, by its very conspicuousness, is openly declared. Both poems serve similar purposes: they present the reader with a general overview of the entire opus; offer the prevailing tone of the work; define the audience and its expectations; and, finally, allude to the poet's current status and point of view. Stampa was far from unique in her remake of this sonnet; most Renaissance *canzonieri* began with a similar paraphrase. The two poems initiate with a direct address to the readers, or listeners:

> Voi, ch'ascoltate in queste meste rime,/. . . il suon . . . (Stampa I)
> (You, who listen to the sound in these melancholy rhymes . . .)

> Voi, ch'ascoltate in rime sparse il suono (Petrarca I)
> (You, who listen to the sound in these scattered rhymes . . .)

The salutation is followed by other recollections of the source: the audience listens to Gaspara's "amorous accents" and her tales of "suffering," or to Francesco's "sighs," born of love; the master hopes to find compassion as well as forgiveness—"spero trovar pietà, non che perdono"—from his readers, while Stampa seeks glory, as well as forgiveness: "gloria, non che perdon . . ./spero trovar."

It is evident that this first Stampian composition intends to establish a direct parallel with the Petrarchan *Canzoniere*. She is informing her readers that she is about to construct an exemplary love story of her own, which is to be compared to the master's work. The borrowings make it quite clear that this will be a collection of poems following the established pattern set two hundred years earlier. This avowal of emulation has two effects on the public. First of all, the reader is reminded of the source, whose contents, themes, messages, and atmosphere are thus transferred to the new work, enriching it with suggestions and echoes of the old. And, second, any direct confrontation of the two texts will emphasize the differences as well as the similarities. Stampa immediately offers her audience variations on the model, making it clear that she is not copying but connoting.

Petrarca's first sonnet establishes the psychological conflict which will dominate his *Canzoniere*, but also gives a conclusive statement of position. The poet declares his love *vano*, that is to say, derived from *vanitas*, futility, shame, and human frailty, concluding that "human pleasures are but brief dreams." From the outset, the Petrarchan reader is forewarned of the poet's final moral outlook, which elects the victory of the spirit over matter, repentence over love. Shame, error, and regret are the keys to the proper interpretation of the *Canzoniere* offered by this prefatory sonnet. None of this moral or religious quandary exists in Stampa's composition. The key to her poetry is provided in the repeated term *mesto*, "melancholy"; she seeks not compassion but glory among the "well-born folk," as well as the envy of other women. Gaspara's introductory sonnet is an exaltation of love, rather than its denigration. There is no repentence for the error of her ways, but a continued hymn to the superiority of the beloved, the "sublime" cause of her torments, which she welcomes for they derive from "such a noble lord." Thus, while initiating her *Rime* with evident borrowings from Petrarca, Stampa alters the model's premises while retaining his vocabulary and imagery. She has achieved a variation on the poet, as suggested in Bembo's theoretical writings, joining creativity to imitation.

This process of creative imitation founded on direct borrowings from the master is carried out elsewhere in a numbe of Stampian compositions. Very often, the first line or commencement is an exact replica of Petrarchan expressions, rather than a simple paraphrase, as in poem CLXXXII:

> La vita fugge, ed io pur sospirando
> trapasso, lassa, il più degli anni miei
> (Life flies and even as I sigh, I pass through most of
> my years, alas.)

> La vita fugge e non s'arresta un'ora
> e la morte vien dietro a gran giornate (CCLXXII)
> (Life flies and stops not an hour, and death follows
> quickly with great forced marches.)

Both poems reflect feelings of loss and dismay caused by the passing of time. The model, however, is preoccupied with the torments created by the imminence of death and the loss of his spiritual guide, Laura. Stampa transforms the Petrarchan original by altering the role of time's passage. As in the prefatory sonnets, the premises are changed and the religious inspiration of the model gives way to a more earthbound motivation. The presence of death and its approach figure prominently in both poems, but Stampa's anxiety and dismay result not from the fear of dying but from the material consequences of time's motion; her lover will leave her, she will lose all her joys. Whereas Petrarca regrets the loss of time in transient pleasures, Stampa regrets the loss of pleasure in the transience of time: "Trapasso, lassa, il piú degli anni miei,/né di passarli ardendo mi dorrei" ("I pass through most of my years, alas, but I would not grieve to spend them burning with love"). Thus, Petrarca's poem of moral angst becomes a complaint against the fleeting nature of love. This thematic incongruity between the two poems is further heightened by another direct linguistic borrowing in the same composition. Stampa's fifth verse echoes Petrarca's seventh line:

> se non che non so punto il come o 'l quando
> den le mie gioie dar luogo agli omei . . . (Stampa)
> (but for the fact that I can't possibly know how or
> when my joys must give way to cries of woe . . .)

se non ch'i' ò di me stesso pietate
i' sarei già di questi pensier fora.
(but for the fact that I have pity for my soul, I'd
have put an end to these thoughts and been free.)

The source subtly introduces the rejection of self-inflicted death on Christian grounds, whereas Stampa's conversion of the original's meaning introduces the negative aspects of her personal situation, a completely temporal one, which do not permit the realization of her hopes of living ardently. In short, Stampa has divested her borrowings of the religious and moral implications inherent in the Petrarchan prototype, substituting a far more secular approach to reality which is indicative of her time. Petrarca could not traverse two centuries unscathed. Indeed, the theme of suicide touched upon by Petrarca in "La vita fugge" is given an unexpected turn by the Renaissance poet. Removed from the Christian context suicide can no longer connote divine displeasure or suggest the eternal suffering of spiritual death. Stampa places the theme in the environment of her self-image. But continuing to represent herself as an inferior being and a possession of the beloved, she negates her own independence. It is not God she will displease or disobey by killing herself, but her earthly lord: "tu non sei tua, tu sei del tuo signore, . . ./l'anima e 'l corpo, e la morte e la vita/divenne sua, e a lui conven che ceda" (LXXXV) ("You are not your own, you are your lord's . . . your soul and body, death and life became his, and must be yielded him").

A similar comparison-contrast is carried out in poem CLI of the *Rime,* which also begins with a Petrarchan commencement:

Piangete, donne, e con voi pianga Amore,
poi che non piange lui, che m'ha ferita
sì, che l'alma farà tosto partita
da questo corpo tormentato fuore.
(Ladies, weep, and Love will weep with
you, for he does not weep, he who so
injured me that my soul will soon depart
from this tormented heart.)

Piangete, donne e con voi pianga Amore,
piangete, amanti, per ciascun paese,
poi ch'è morto colui . . . (Petrarca XCII)
(Ladies, weep, and Love will weep with
you; weep, lovers, everywhere, for he is
dead . . .)

The Petrarchan sonnet is an invitation to women and lovers to mourn
the death of the great lyric poet, Cino da Pistoia. Stampa's poem also
deals with death and mourning, but the deceased is the poet herself,
killed by her beloved's indifference. This theme is, in itself, Petrarchan. The themes of the earlier sonnet are poetry, love, death, and
mourning. Stampa retains these subjects, modifying them to suit her
own purpose. Whereas the original had been a eulogy to honor the
celebrated poet of love, Cino, now gone to heaven, leaving desolation
in the hearts of ladies, lovers, Petrarca, poetry, and his native Pistoia,
Gaspara's imitation mourns her own demise—the victim of unhappy
love—only to conclude with an actual epitaph, presented in the tercets,
to be chiseled on her grave marker: " 'Per amar molto ed esser poco
amata/visse e morì infelice, ed or qui giace/la più fidel amante che sia
stata' " ("For having much loved and being loved little, she lived and
died unhappily, and now the most faithful lover that ever was rests
here").[9] Changed in this manner, the Petrarchan encomium on the
death of a poet of love becomes an epitaph for the poet herself because
of love. The theme appeals to Stampa, for poem LXXXVI is
introduced by the same borrowed opening: "Piangete, donne, e poi
che la mia morte" ("Ladies, weep for my death"). And it too
concludes with a short epitaph for "the unhappy and loyal Anassilla,"
who died owing to the cruelty of her lover. Both Stampian sonnets
enter the realm of death fantasy, so well expressed by the master in
such celebrated poems as "Chiare fresche e dolci acque."
    Stampa's Petrarchan borrowings are not limited to first verses, but
they can be found throughout the poetry, with similar functions of
suggestion, comparison, differentiation, and variation on a theme.[10]
Although not as powerfully allusive as they might be at the beginning
of a composition, these extracted phrases still exert a significant

connotative force. For example, in poem XCVI of the *Rime* there are
two slightly altered passages culled from the *Canzoniere:*

> com'io vorrei, tanto 'l disio mi sprona (Stampa, v. 3)
> (. . . as I would like, for desire spurs me on so.)
>
> fuggo ove 'l gran desio mi sprona . . . (Petrarca, CLI, v. 4)
> (I fly where my great desire spurs me on . . .)
>
> rompa per la pietate i duri sassi (v. 14)
> (out of pity, it breaks hard stones)
>
> devrian de la pietà romper un sasso (CCXCIV, v. 7)
> (out of pity, they should even break a stone)

Stampa's sonnet describes her wish to be with the beloved, spurred on
by the desire for union; their separation is so painful, that her sorrow
would make even stones break out of pity for her. The second of the
models from the *Canzoniere* is also a poem of separation; it is the
poet's longing soul and the voice of deprived Love that sound such
piteous laments. Thus, the two sonnets complement each other, the
sorrow of one echoing the pain of the other. On the other hand, the
first borrowing is derived from a sonnet which rejoices in the pain of
love, inflicted by the beloved's eyes, from which his every thought of
love and his every inspiration come. Stampa fuses the two Petrarchan
notions—painful separation and joyful pain—into a composition built
on a martial theme: they are separated by war and she would be with
him to shield him with her very body. The tension of the Stampian
work originates in a typically Petrarchan frustration: the insufficiency
of loving and willing. It is then materialized in the military imagery of
her own, which elicits scenes of combat and aggression against her
count. Thus, the tone is partially rendered through the borrowings,
but then represented in the battle scene, only to return to the frustrated
psyche of the poet, a frustration emphasized by the impenetrability of
the final image of the "hard stones," which cannot be broken by pity
any more than her desire can achieve their reunion. The examples
from the *Rime* could be greatly expanded to include dozens of lines,

half-lines, and altered verses that the disciple borrowed from the master's *Canzoniere*, but they would simply reiterate the conclusions drawn from these limited samples. Petrarca afforded a well-stocked hunting ground for literary depredation and the poets of the late Italian Renaissance were good poachers.

"But it was everyone's complete and honest belief that the language of poetry, particularly that of love poetry (and all loves) was by then—consecrated, inviolable, unchangeable—Petrarca's, so that collections of phrases and idioms and adjectivation from the *Canzoniere* were assembled in a kind of poetic-amorous dictionary."[11] Word choice was suggested by the Petrarchan vocabulary, so that it too became something to imitate. Stampa's selection of certain specific terms was determined not by contemporary speech but by lyric tradition. A number of words were defined by Petrarchan usage. A prime example is *sole*, literally meaning "sun." Through poetic application it had come to signify the beloved, Christ, a heavenly guide, or the eyes of the loved one; it was used to describe spiritual leadership, guidance, and elevation. Allied to this term, there existed a whole series of associated solar images: ray, light, lamp, flame, fire, beam, and so forth. Eye imagery was especially popular and closely related to notions of illumination. Eyes were alternately lights, suns, lamps, flames, spheres, and trusted guides. A *laccio* was occasionally a snare, ambush, or rope but more often referred to the bonds of love; *noia* was not boredom but pain and suffering; *l'età fiorita* was a metaphor for youth, "the age in flower," while the *mortal velo*, "mortal veil," represented the human body; *sdegno* was not necessarily disdain but often an act against *pietà*, "compassion" or "pity"; *chiaro* did not suppose brightness but clarity, luminescence, nobility, and distinction; *vago* generally implied a desirous or restless state rather than obscurity or vagueness. The list could be extended considerably but it is distinguished by a predilection for general terms which possess an allusive and ineffable quality difficult to achieve when employing more exact terminology.

In addition to the Petrarchan vocabulary, Stampa also employed his forms, and sought to imitate his style and rhetorical devices. The Italian or Petrarchan sonnet was the most popular poetic structure adopted by sixteenth-century lyric poets. It is composed of two quatrains, followed by two tercets. The meter is the Italian hendeca-syllable, or eleven-syllable line, with irregularly set accents and pauses. Gaspara Stampa invariably used the rhyme scheme ABBA in the quatrains and, while tercets generally have a looser rhyme combination than allowed in the first two stanzas, Stampa preferred the fixed scheme CDCDCD for her sonnets. Their syntactic structure is similar to Petrarca's. The quatrains are preparatory and much more slowly paced than the tercets; they tend to present the descriptive element of the poem or develop a situation, which is then concluded in the more rapid movement of the tercets. The first two stanzas generally introduce situations or feelings in a detailed depiction which unfolds in a relatively subdued descriptive way. The quatrains are then set against the concentrated nature of the closing stanzas where the subjective voice of the *persona* vibrates more intensely and ardently.[12]

Due to its length, the sonnet offers an ideal form for the presentation of emotions or emotional situations. It is sufficiently long to be descriptive and dramatic but a bit too short to be employed for narration. Stampa utilized it well to express the workings of her artistic *anima*. The rhythmic possibilities offered by the repetition of sounds in the end rhymes could be reinforced by other sound patterns experimented successfully by the model: assonance, alliteration, con-sonance, internal rhyme, anaphora, repetition, and refrain. Other devices associated with Petrarca include the extensive use of rhetorical questions, invocation, antithesis, oxymoron, allegory, metaphor, and parallel constructions. The detailed analysis of poem CXI of the *Rime* is indicative of the manner in which Stampa integrated the master's poetic idiom:

> Pommi ove 'l mar irato geme e frange,
> ov'ha l'acqua più queta e più tranquilla;
> pommi ove 'l sol più arde e più sfavilla,
> o dove il ghiaccio altrui trafige ed ange;
>   pommi al Tanai gelato, al freddo Gange,
> ove dolce rugiada e manna stilla,
> ove per l'aria empio velen scintilla,
> o dove per amor si ride e piange;
>   pommi ove 'l crudo Scita ed empio fere,

> o dove è queta gente e riposata,
> o dove tosto o tardi uom vive e pere:
> vivrò qual vissi, e sarò qual son stata,
> pur che le fide mie due stelle vere
> non rivolgan da me la luce usata.

(Ah set me where the angry sea wails and breaks, where the waters
are most calm and tranquil; ah set me where the sun blazes and
shines the most, or where ice pierces and torments others; ah set me
in the frozen Don or in the cold Ganges, where sweet balms and
manna ooze, where evil poisons sparkle in the air, and where one
laughs and weeps for love; ah set me where the cruel and godless
Scythian strikes, or where calm and undisturbed people are, or
where sooner or later man lives and dies: I'll live as I've lived, I'll
be as I was, as long as my own two loyal stars do not turn away
their wonted light.)

The inspiration for this sonnet is another Petrarchan source, "Pommi
ove 'l sole" (CXLV). The two poems share a common theme: no
matter where the lover is in space or time, he will never change his
feelings. Stylistically, Stampa's major anaphora is formed with the
imperative *pommi* ("ah set me") which is repeated at the beginning of
the first, third, fifth, and ninth verses. Petrarca had employed the
expression six times to Stampa's four, but the Renaissance poet adds a
second anaphora construction with the repetitions of *ove, ov'ha,* and *o
dove,* which are also used in connection with the first, original
anaphora, *pommi ove.* The source of this secondary anaphora is the
second line of the Petrarchan sonnet, but the model does not utilize
this repetition beyond the first quatrain. Only Stampa's final tercet is
totally free of this rhetorical figure. Sound patterns are formed by the
prevalence of vowel sounds which echo throughout the composition.
Certain words are also repeated, forming internal bonds which unify
the poem, notably *queta* and *empio,* which present slightly divergent
meanings as they reappear. People and waters are not calm in the
same fashion, while a poison cannot be godless although a Scythian
might well be evil; however, the context seems to imply the savagery
generally associated with this ethnic group. The recurrence of words
leads to a play on verbal tenses which is also present in the model:

> sarò qual fui, vivrò com'io son visso (Petrarca, v. 13)
> (I will be as I was, I'll live as I lived)

> vivrò qual vissi, e sarò qual son stata (Stampa, v. 12)
> (I'll live as I lived, I'll be as I was)

Stampa merely transposes the sequence in which the verbs appear, thus altering the past tenses, a process visible in the Italian but difficult to note in an English translation.

Another familiar feature of Petrarchan syntax is a procedure occasionally termed plurality, which is the tendency to distribute the thought or expression of a composition into a multipartite structure, so that each speech fragment is multiplied in various parts lined up on the same semantic axis.[13] For example, a number of different adjectives or verbs will be employed to describe a noun or action; these terms do not necessarily have a referential function but merely serve to create a specific cadence or rhythm in the verse. In this poem, Stampa uses plurality to give a certain harmony to her lines. The waters are both calm and tranquil, the people calm and undisturbed; little meaning separates the two adjectives in either case but their doubling serves to give a measured tempo to the verse. This same cadence is achieved by the doubling of verbs in each phrase: the sun both blazes and shines, ice pierces and torments, the sea wails and breaks, and so on. Nouns are also doubled, as in the case of the two rivers, the Don and Ganges, which are described with two similar adjectives, frozen and cold. Rarely, in either Renaissance lyric poetry or in Petrarca, is a single adjective used. The tendency is to accumulate in order to create rhythmic patterns.

This typical multipartite structure is indicative of another related rhetorical device: antithesis. Rather than being similar in meaning, the speech patterns are in opposition: "one laughs and weeps," "sooner or later," "man lives and dies." In this particular sonnet, and in many others, antithesis extends beyond semantic elements, such as plurality, and enters into the actual denotation of the terms. Liquid and solid elements are contrasted (sea, water, sun, ice), heat and cold (sun, ice, and accompanying verbs, cold rivers), motion and stillness (wails and breaks, calm and tranquil), violence and tranquillity (the godless

Scythian, the quiet people), life and death. The final tercet offers a solution to the antithetical nature of the former eleven verses by resolving the issue through the comparison of verb tenses: the present belongs to her own loyal stars, while she is and exists in the past and future. Meaning is conveyed through grammar: she will love stead-fastly throughout time, as long as her beloved continues to reciprocate her devotion.

Most cases of multipartite constructions tend to triple and even quadruple the elements involved, rather than merely doubling them as in *Pommi ove 'l mar*. Stampa utilizes this extended plurality in a variety of semantic situations and with various parts of speech. The effect is that of a list. But it is a poetic list where words are strung together for their pleasing harmonies. The quatrains from poem **XXVI** demonstrate the lavish linguistic redundancy that can be obtained:

> Arsi, piansi, cantai; piango, ardo e canto;
> piangerò, arderò, canterò sempre
> (fin che Morte o Fortuna o tempo stempre
> a l'ingegno, occhi e cor, stil, foco e pianto)
> la bellezza, il valor e 'l senno a canto,
> che 'n vaghe, sagge ed onorate tempre
> Amor, natura e studio par che tempre
> nel volto, petto e cor del lume santo.

(I burned, wept, sang; I weep, burn and sing; I will always weep and burn and sing [until Death or Fate or time dissolve in my mind, eyes and heart, style, fire and tears] his beauty, valor and wisdom as well, that Love, nature and art appear to mold in the countenance, breast and heart of this blessed light and in all pleasing, sage and honored characters.)

Multipartite verbal units dominate the first and second verses, while noun groupings are preeminent throughout the quatrains and only one adjectival clause is present. The first line is distinctive because of the emphatic caesura which breaks the rhythmical flow of the hendecasyl-lable; the semicolons function as grammatical and musical pauses, separating this first line of verse from the sound pattern established in the other seven. The poet is emphasizing the melodious character of her discourse, first by the staccato movement of the commencement; each verb is a separate two-syllable unit, set apart by both punctuation and pronunciation. The seven lines that follow, however, form a lyric movement initiated by the introduction of the future tense and the adverb "always." Both convey an open-end quality which is accentuated by the lengthened words, concluding in the "o" sound. The piling up of terms then proceeds in a cumulative verbal crescendo which terminates in the words *lume santo,* a metaphor for the beloved, who is thus exceptionally gifted with the amassed wordage.

Besides her skill at the musical orchestration, Stampa also carried out knowledgeable technical refinements, such as the use of equivocal rhyme, employed when the same word is used with two different meanings. *Canto* in line 1 has the significance of "I sing" and is a present tense verb, whereas in line 5 it can be translated as "as well," although it is literally "beside," an adverb. The same technique is employed in verses 6 and 7 with the word *tempre,* which is alternately a noun and a verb. Similarly, the noun *pianto,* weeping or tears, has the same etymology as the verbs *piansi, piango,* and *piangerò,* serving as an echo in the sound pattern of the quatrains.

Another rhetorical technique characteristic of Renaissance poetry in general and Stampa's *Rime* in particular is the regular use of antithesis and oxymoron. A celebrated feature of Petrarca's *Canzoniere,* these devices serve thematic as well as stylistic functions. In the poetic idiom of the day, antithesis represented the conflictual nature of love, such as the coexistence of opposite emotions like love and hate, ardor and indifference, rejoicing and depression. Through antithesis, the psychological reality of a feeling could be expressed semantically in the language of contrasts. Gaspara Stampa took full advantage of this traditional technique to give voice to her own internal strife, as well as the contradictory temperament of the beloved. Thus, through the emulation of the model, she was able to fuse her personal content and poetic discourse. Many of the oppositions employed were an integral part of the Petrarchan vocabulary, such as the contrasts between life and death, sweetness and bitterness, peace and war, joy and pain, heat and cold:

I am fire and you are ice,
you are free and I'm in chains. (XLI)

I hate who loves me and love who scorns me. (XLIII)

And so life and death, and joys and pains,
and dread and confidence, and war and peace,
all come from you, Love, from a single place. (CLXIII)

An occasional oxymoron is also added to Stampa's application of the
antithetical constructions popularized through Petrarchan imitation:
"O bitter joy, o my sweet torment" (LXXVI).

Other rhetorical devices also serve to express emotion, thought,
reactions, and explosions of feeling. Gaspara prefers interjection,
apostrophe, repetition, and rhetorical questions. Used as outbursts of
feeling, the exclamations represent cries of distress or need, as well as
vocalizations of hope, worry, devotion, and satisfaction. Interjections
are far more frequent in Stampa than they are in Petrarca. Eleven
sonnets in the *Rime* begin with *Deh* ("ah! pray!") compared to three
in the *Canzoniere;* another eleven commence with *O* while the
expressions *ahimé, oimé,* and *lassa* ("alas!" "poor me!") appear often
throughout the poems. Imperative constructions are fairly common, as
are parenthetical remarks and asides. Occasionally entire quatrains are
composed of rhetorical questions, joined to other devices of poetic
diction:

> Ma che, sciocca, dich'io? perché vaneggio?
> (two rhetorical questions and a personal aside)
> perché sì sfuggo questo chiaro inganno?
> (iteration of *perché,* symmetrical construction,
>   rhetorical question, oxymoron)
> perché sgravarmi da sì util danno,
> (anaphora, oxymoron)
> pronta ne' danni miei, ad Amor chieggio?
> (repetition of the *p-r* sounds, internal rhyme
>   with *danno-danni,* rhetorical question)
> (LXXXIX)

(Fool, what am I saying? why am I raving? why am I fleeing such
a noble delusion? why, content in my own injuries, ask Love to free
me of such beneficial injury?)

Many of Stampa's symbols, metaphors, and similes are also derived
from Francesco Petrarca's lyric storehouse. One recurring image in
both poets is that of the beloved's eyes. Traditionally, these represent
spiritual guides—the lover's "suns," "lamps," "stars," and "lights"—
to direct the poetic *persona* to higher aspirations. They can also be
windows into the soul and thoughts of the beloved, as well as mirrors
of an elevated spiritual world. The lover may turn to them for comfort
and guidance: "I run to you, blessed and divine lights, to you who are
my trusted guides" (CXLIV). On occasion, the eyes have negative
connotations: they are beautiful but distant and unattainable; the lover
cannot interpret their message; they remind one of the suffering and
frustration associated with unreturned passion. Often, both Petrarca
and Stampa employ the eyes as a synecdoche for the person of the
beloved, as in Gaspara's sonnet "Quando innanti ai begli occhi"
("When I come before those beautiful, immortal, bright eyes"). Often
the disciple employs the eyes as only one of the symbols in a larger,
extended metaphor made popular by the master and exploited by the
lyric poets of the sixteenth century.

The imagery of this extended metaphor is complex: life is a sea in
which the soul of the lover is a small boat, caught in the tempests of
doubt or inner strife; fearing the dangers of the reefs, which are
symbols of temptation, the boat seeks safe moorings in the harbor,
love or God, but cannot reach port because it lacks a helmsman or
guide, the beloved or his/her eyes. It was a theme particularly dear to
religious poets, such as Vittoria Colonna, who could associate love for
a human with love for the divine, transforming the beloved into a
celestial intermediary. Naturally, Collaltino becomes Gaspara's guide,
her "stars," in a number of compositions based on this metaphor. One
poem, LXXII, is a variation on the Petrarchan allegory: her life is a
sea, its waters her tears, the winds her sighs, the ship her hope, the sail
and oars her desires. The religious symbolism is lost, however. As is
common in Stampa's variations on Petrarca, it is an ambiguous
reworking of the master's themes. The storms are no longer a

metaphor for sin or earthly temptations but become "my fears and cold jealousies, slow to go and quick to appear." The allegory is not indicative of a separation from God or righteousness, but of a sundering from the beloved. There are no lulls in her stormy life since the count left her, taking all her "hours of serenity." As is often the case, Stampa's inspiration is far more secular than religious.

Some of Stampa's borrowings from Petrarca are merely superficial reproductions which add little to either her *Rime* or Francesco's fame, a case in point being the canzone "Chiaro e famoso mare," openly modeled after "Chiare fresche e dolci acque." It is a poor variant at best, lacking in originality and character. In general, Stampa is a lesser poet than Petrarca, lacking his ability to present a perfect harmonious composition. This disciple does not have the refined touch of the master, his sense of polished elegance, his well-turned phrase, and formal training. Nor are the imitative works among Stampa's best creations. They do serve, however, to place her in a historical and literary context, to specify her position in Italian literature, to define her debt to tradition, and to reveal her sources, interests, and aspirations. But, even as a Petrarchan imitator, Gaspara Stampa occasionally adds a new touch, a novel approach, a subtle alteration. And within the variations on the themes and language of the model, the poet must also seek her own voice, that of a woman.

The Feminine Voice

One of the peculiarities of sixteenth-century poetry was the presence of so many women writers. Almost all were *petrarchisti,* seeking to imitate the psychological complexities and human experiences of a man in their own poetry. These female poets were forced to modify the Petrarchan and Bembian formulas to suit their different situation. As a woman poet, Stampa had to deal with some profound issues. As a female, how was she to present herself in the active role of lover and admirer? Even though he was a man, the beloved would have to be placed in the passive role as the recipient of love. Images, symbols, and metaphors had to be found to reflect the feminine condition. In short, Stampa had to find a means of presenting the male-female love relationship in feminine terms when the existing vocabulary was masculine. One solution was to simply not distinguish between the sexual roles. Some women poets, such as Vittoria Colonna and Veronica Gambara, merely accepted the traditional poetic idiom without substantial alterations. Curiously, their poetry was and is generally regarded as "virile." This adjective is never applied to Gaspara Stampa. Both her biographical commentators and literary critics insist on her femininity, which surfaces even in the context of obvious borrowings from Petrarca.

One evident disadvantage of conventional lyric poetry is its lack of masculine appellations. Women could be addressed as *signora* and *donna*, both titles of respect suffused with a subtle erotic undertone. A man could not be called *uomo*, the exact equivalent of *donna*, for it was not a term of address. Stampa occasionally employs *signore*, loosely translatable as lord, but the word possesses social and religious connotations, being often used in reference to God or to a superior. Lovers, according to literary custom, were presumed equals, at least in matters of love, which knew no social or class barriers but followed its own laws. As Maria Bellonci has pointed out, the title *conte*, "count," admirably filled the poet's needs. It was a match in sound, syllable count, and tone for the Petrarchan *donna*, "woman" or "lady." Unlike *signore*, *conte* was void of any reverential meaning and could be used when reproaching, demanding, pleading, exalting, and praising.

Besides his title, Collaltino di Collalto also provided a name which was an ideal counterpart to that of Petrarca's lady, Laura. Her emblematic name could be transfigured upon demand into other allusive nouns: *l'aura* ("air"), *l'auro* ("gold"), and *lauro* ("laurel tree," the symbol of poetry sacred to Apollo; "laurel wreath," symbol of glory). Collaltino di Collalto is not a melodious name, lacking the rich sound qualities and allegorical potential of "Laura" but it had considerable poetic possibilities for Stampa, who metamorphosed it into *colle* ("hill") and, by extension, Parnassus and Helicon, the former being the sacred hill and the latter the home of Apollo and the Muses. The allegoric name thus obtained designates the love relationship; the count becomes a height to conquer, a sacred resting place, and her poetic muse. In the plural, *colli* is used to symbolize his domain, a natural setting which alternately represents the protagonist's amorous fulfillment or painful separation from the beloved, creating symbolic and physical barriers between them.

Elevation is implicit in any hill, being at once physical, emotional, cultural, and spiritual where Collaltino is concerned. In Stampa's allegory, he becomes a height to conquer or to gaze upon in wonder. The properties of shadiness and restfulness attributed to hills are also worked into the imagery. Stampa's poetic *persona* literally walks in his fertilizing shade. Her "verdant, excellent and great hill" has a characteristic akin to Petrarca's laurel: the power to radiate poetic inspiration, this sacred shade ".... raises me from a lowly place, renews my style, suggests my vein; it always arouses such virtue in my soul!" (III). The image of a lofty hill also befits the celebration of a virile warrior. Collaltino's allegoric appellation allows the introduction of the traits of strength and power, mitigated by the knightly virtues of gentility and courtesy. He is transformed into a shelter for the lover, where the weak woman can find protection and rest, "where resting I await the crown, sweet repose from my labors" (X). To these characteristics, Stampa also adds the power to produce life and to fertilize (the verdant foliage covering the hill) as well as the masculine trait of ruling from a position of dominion. This symbolic depiction of Collaltino emphasizes his potency, ascendancy, and fecundity, evoking Stampa's declarations on the power of the beloved to motivate her art. Poetry emanates through him and Amore, while she is an inferior instrument. Magnified in the love rapport, the traditional male and female roles, in which the woman literally and figuratively looks up to her man, finds its mode of expression in Petrarchan antithesis: " 'Non son,' mi dice Amor, 'le ragione pari;/egli è nobile e bel, tu brutta e vile;/egli larghi, tu hai li cieli avari./Gioia e tormento al merto tuo simile/convien ch'io doni.' " ("Love tells me: 'The sides are uneven; he is noble and handsome, you are ugly and base; his skies are generous, yours miserly. It's best I grant you joy and torment equal to your worth,' " CL).

The sexual and personal abyss separating the two protagonists of this *canzoniere* fuels the existing *topos* of the cruel lover in Stampa's *Rime*. The theme was already present in Petrarca but is greatly expanded by Stampa. The early mentions of the count's indifference and aloofness are soon aggravated and aggrandized. Even the positive metaphor of the sun-eyes is altered; the poet shifts from praising her "stars" to acrimoniously denouncing them. In an impetus of despair, the lover paints a sadistic portrait of Collaltino's eyes, which are no longer the portals to his soul or the guides to serenity, notwithstanding their deceptive appearance:

> Quando sarete mai sazie e satolle
> del lungo strazio mio, de le mie pene,
> luci, assai piú che 'l sol chiare e serene?
> . . . .
> Quando fia che vi vegga un dì pietose,
> e duri la pietà vostra, e non manchi
> tosto, come le lievi e frali cose? (XXXIII)

(When will my torments and my pain satisfy and sate you, oh lights, you who are much clearer and more serene than the sun? . . . Will the day come when you will be piteous and not fail me at once, as do delicate and frail things?)

The eyes, like the beloved, can change their nature from life-giving to death-producing. Stampa's response to unhappiness and unfulfilled love is similar to Petrarca's; she invokes death as her salvation and release, the only liberation from her unbearable pain. Death holds no fears for Gaspara; it is "everlasting night" (XCV) where "one can suddenly end all suffering" (CLXXXV). Stampa does not share Petrarca's preoccupation with divine justice and eternal damnation. Death appears only as peace and escape.

Another popular aspect derived from the *Canzoniere* is the presence of anniversary poems in the *Rime*. These are celebrations or evocations of the first meeting of the lovers. In both poets, the remembrance is fraught with symbolism. Petrarca made much of his encounter with Laura on Good Friday, for it emblematized his inability to choose between worldly and divine love. Gaspara Stampa's first anniversary or encounter sonnet proposes a different religious observance, one of the happier events of the liturgical calendar, in keeping with the positive depiction of her love offered by the prefatory sonnet: "The day drew near when the Creator, who could have remained in his grandeur, came to show himself in human form" (II). Christ's birth signals the transformation of the deity into human flesh. God has become man to save all people. The poet uses this sacred event to draw a parallel between God's choice to enter a woman's body and the count's choice to love her. Like Mary, she dutifully accepts an honor far superior to her innate worthiness. Just as Mary became the receptacle of divine love made man, Gaspara becomes the receptacle of a superior love:

> . . . degnò l'illustre mio signore,
> per cui ho tanti poi lamenti sparsi,
> potendo in luogo più alto annidarsi,
> farsi nido e ricetto del mio core.
> Ond'io sì rara e sì alta ventura
> accolsi lieta. . . .

(Although he might have found a higher place to nest, my illustrious lord, for whom I later shed so many tears, deigned to make a nest and shelter of my heart. And I joyfully welcomed so rare and so great a fortune. . . .)

Whereas Petrarca chose to celebrate a feast of death, Gaspara's choice reflects a very different allegorical context rendered with a feminine viewpoint. Naturally, the elements of conception, pregnancy, and birth reflect a woman's reality. But the images also tell more: the poet views herself as a shelter, a nest, a home; her love is maternal, tender, and depicts two typically feminine endeavors, the giving of life and its nurturing. Having to write within a conventional mold, Stampa has utilized it but also transformed it to suit her femininity and the passivity generally attributed to woman's nature. The image of maternity, emphasized by the accompanying "nest" and "heart," describes the reception of love and offers a solution to her artistic dilemma. In her dual role of lover, thus responsible for singing the praises of the beloved, and woman, Stampa must find an adequate symbol of both passivity and activity. Maternity offers the solution. She receives love on the one hand, but also gives life. It is also a metaphor for the creative act of composing poetry, urged on by the inspiration of love.

The remaining anniversary poems are modeled on Petrarca but retain the positive qualities associated with a feast of birth; Christmas

is a time of happiness, rejoicing, generosity, and joy. These characteristics, tempered by signs of unhappiness, dominate these sonnets. The
second anniversary poem meets the event with declarations of unqual-
ified acceptance of the "amorous snare," set by a matchless "beauty":
"I regret nothing, nay, I glory and rejoice; ... I welcome this
amorous flame and this chill" (CLV). The poems reiterate Stampa's
readiness to love, as presented in the *ancilla Domini* theme of the first
anniversary sonnet, expressing willing and fatalistic submission to
another's will. Another poem written in commemoration, if not
celebration, of the second year of love suggests moral contrition and
sorrow due to its manifest allusion to Petrarca's famous "Padre del
ciel": "Father in heaven, you see with how much pain Love and fever
come to torment this miserable spirit and this shell" (CLIX). The
Petrarchan sonnet was composed on the eleventh year of his passion;
it is a plaintive request for pardon and divine help to return to the
Christian way of life. The commencement, as reproduced by Stampa
as well, is a reference to the beginning of the "Our Father, who art in
heaven." Once again, the religious implications are generally ignored
by Stampa. Her pain is twofold: a feverish state and the fever of love.
Her prayer is not redemptive or contrite; it is a request to God to
"extinguish" one or the other of her feverish tormentors. She pleads
for strength, protection, and paternal solicitude, but not for moral
direction. Fever has supplanted Petrarca's infernal "harsh adversary."
The devil's traps give way to Love's subtle weapons. Stampa adheres
to the stereotype of feminine weakness, appealing to a strong male—
here in divine garb—to sustain her, a "weak woman with very little
strength." The final anniversary poem, CCIX, is an acknowledgment
of the continuing power of love after three years' passing, but, just as
a spiritualized image of Collaltino has replaced his physical presence,
so too rational love has overcome its sensual counterpart. The memory
of "two beautiful eyes and a smile" and the sting of an "ancient love"
remain, but they have been attenuated if not forgotten. No other
anniversary poems were to follow.

It is in the act of loving and artistically voicing her psyche that
Stampa comes closest in inspiration to Francesco Petrarca. Her poetry,
like his, is the realization of the encounter of the subject with himself,
a product of consciousness, self-awareness, and continuous soul-search-

ing into the inner recesses of emotion and thought. Both poets are primarily interested in the description of self and, second, in the discussion of love.

In the *Rime* love causes torments and pain but it is never completely rejected by the *persona*. Even the religious sonnets of contrition, while accepting the Petrarchan formula of avowed prostration and torpor, never deny the presence and value of love. The "Rime d'Amore" are compact in their intensity. Nothing veers the reader from the thematic core: the multifaceted nature of love and lovers. Petrarca's love poetry is integrated into a diversified work which includes compositions that transfer the attention of his public to other matters; correspondence sonnets, invectives against cleric corruption, and political works take away the reader's focus from the love story. For example, the celebrated sonnet "Benedetto sia 'l giorno e 'l mese e l'anno" (*Canzoniere* LXI) is a paean to love and all its effects, including the sweet pain, sighs, tears, desires, and his rhymes. The resulting mood is tempered, however, by the juxtaposition of "Padre del ciel," which immediately follows. By placing the two sonnets together, Petrarca imposes an inevitable comparison; the exaltation of love is mitigated by the awareness of death, sin, and the miseries of spiritual subjugation to venery. There are no moderating juxtapositions to diminish the power of Stampa's benedicite to love's pain and joyous suffering:

> Io benedico, Amor, tutti gli affanni,
> tutte le ingiurie e tutte le fatiche,
> tutte le noie novelle ed antiche,
> che m'hai fatto provar tante e tanti anni;
>   benedico le frodi e i tanti inganni,
> con che convien che i tuoi seguaci intriche;
> poi che tornando le due stelle amiche
> m'hanno in un tratto ristorati i danni. (CIII)

(Love, I bless every anguish, every outrage, and every labor, every past and present worry, with which you've tried me so much for so many years. I bless the tricks and many deceits you must use to entangle your following; for since their return, my two propitious stars have instantly compensated me for any loss.)

This paean is not attended by any suggestions of repentance, fear, or doubt. Indeed, it is followed by one of the *Rime*'s most openly sensual compositions, "O notte, a me più chiara," a hymn to a happy but all too brief night of love. But Stampa's paean is wrought of pain. The presence of constant suffering forms the underlying atmosphere of the book. The poetic *persona* suffers for love, so that even this pain can be translated into joy. In a subtle fashion, Stampa transmutes anguish into rapture; it becomes a masochistic exercise in the art of loving. The barrier between pleasure and pain is erased and the two blend into the antithetical amalgam which is love.

In Stampian poetry, *amore* is an overwhelming force, whose duration, aggressive persistence, and omnipresent influence can be perceived in the few spiritual sonnets of this Renaissance *canzoniere*. Placed at the end of the *Rime* by Abdelkader Salza, these compositions were to be interpreted as the crowning point of an entire life and literary production, the poet's final message of religious devotion and spiritual urgency. These sonnets also have their source in the Petrarchan model. But in attempting to adapt her voice to the master's, Stampa creates a singular emulative mixture. Petrarca's volume ends with a canzone to the Virgin. Mary, however, is a figure Gaspara associates with herself in the anniversary poems rather than with the deity. The Madonna is therefore replaced with God the Father or, most often, God the Son, her masculine counterparts. The poetic images are familiar implementations of the existing love code. Her "dark and fierce longings" and "vain, false, and weak desire" are the fruit of her love for a "mortal thing" (CCCIV). Declarations of weakness and helplessness alternate with pleas for forgiveness and divine understanding. Stampa's prayers are grounded in impotence and disabled by the ever-present undercurrent of sensuality. Love is not only not conquered, it is not even dully regretted. From the mortal God who gave himself for the salvation of all she implores grace and *virtù*. Her statements, as Donadoni rightly recognized, recall the fatalistic religiosity of Lutheran and Calvinist thought; salvation is to be granted through faith and God's grace, rather than through good works: "Lord, who give and take paradise away, give and take according to our great and little faith (but not according to our works, for they are too weak and foolish to receive such generous mercy)"

(CCCVI).[14] More than aid, Stampa implores the miracle of redemptive grace and the coming of divine goodness. Her God must seek her and does.

Petrarca needed only to look upon the symbol of salvation, the crucifix, to enter into his spiritual morass. Stampa's Christ cries to her from his cross: " 'Turn your eyes to me, godless sinner,' my Lord cries out to me as he hangs upon his cross" (CCCVII). The sinner's eyes are still directed, however, to a "handsome human countenance" (CCV). To this crucified Christ, symbol of mortal suffering, the poet speaks of her own carnal frailty and of the attraction of an unforgettable but all too human love: "the beauty that I love is one of the rarest you have ever made; but since it is terrestial, it cannot equal that of your realm" (CCCVIII). Stampa must struggle to remind herself of God's goodness and man's sinfulness, as her thoughts continue to wander away from the "eternal and celestial" toward the love for a mortal beauty, "as delicate as glass" (CCCX).

Gaspara's repentance is flawed, her contrition incomplete. The search for grace is hampered by the recurring relapses into the temptations of the material world. On occasion the figures of the beloved and the godhead merge, the one substituting for the other. One curious image—an obvious if unwilling allusion to Collaltino—is employed to describe heaven, which is God's "alti, celesti e sacri colli" ("noble, celestial and sacred hills"). Just as many of the love poems were sent to her resistant lover in order to make him return to her from his hills, the religious sonnets plead with the Almighty to visit her with his grace, to come to her with his compassion and kindness. One love supplants the other, both are equally "intense and ardent" (CCCVI), both are dependent upon male condescension. Christ replaces Collaltino as the recipient of her supplications and tears. Yet, true to herself, Stampa requests love of her God, a metaphysical love to replace the physical, an eternal love that will not deceive or abandon her: ". . . so that I may only gaze upon you, love only you, long for you, my glorious, eternal and true aim" (CCCVIII). It is not elevated religious fervor which inspires Stampa's religious sonnets, but the need to find fulfillment, gratification, serenity, and true love. The *Rime* conclude with one of the poet's justifiably famous works, which is in part an imitation of the Petrarchan formulas,[15] but rendered soft, delicate, caressing, feminine, and totally her own:

> Mesta e pentita de' miei gravi errori
> e del mio vaneggiar tanto e sì lieve,
> e d'aver speso questo tempo breve
> de la vita fugace in vani amori,
>   a te, Signor, ch'intenerisci i cori,
> e rendi calda la gelata neve,
> e fai soave ogn'aspro peso e greve
> a chiunque accendi di tuoi santi ardori,
>   ricorro; e prego che mi porghi mano
> a trarmi fuor del pelago, onde uscire,
> s'io tentassi da me, sarebbe vano.
>   Tu volesti per noi, Signor, morire,
> tu ricomprasti tutto il seme umano;
> dolce Signor, non mi lasciar perire!
>   (CCCXI)

(Sad and repentant of my sinful ways, of my many worthless wanderings, of wasting this brief and fleeting life in vain loves, I come to you, Lord, for you can soften any heart and warm the frozen snow, you sweeten every grievous bitter load for those illumined by your holy flame, and I beg you to hold out your hand to me and pull me from these depths, for if I tried it all alone, it would be vain. Lord, you chose to die for us, you redeemed the entire human race; o sweet Lord, do not let me perish!)

Chapter Four

Earthly Venuses and Celestial Counts

The reading and imitation of Francesco Petrarca's *Canzoniere* did not exhaust the Renaissance's fascination with the subject of love. Another source of information and inspiration was the philosophy of Platonism, which had undergone considerable study and reevaluation in fourteenth- and fifteenth-century scholarship. The influence of Neo-Platonism soon spread beyond the limits of academic philosophizing and invaded the territories of lyric poetry, treatises on love, etiquette, and moral reflection. There were strong ties uniting Petrarchismo to Platonism from the start. Petrarca himself had been affected by the discussions on the Greek philosopher which were a common element of Humanist debate, especially due to his friendship for Colluccio Salutati, one of the first fervent admirers of Plato to appear in the Trecento. One of Francesco's regrets was his inability to read the celebrated Greek thinker in the original but only through later commentaries. Petrarca's reverence for Plato was a natural outgrowth of his saturation with the Greco-Roman heritage, but it also reflected a growing public awareness of the ancient thinker's system of ideas. And, on a superficial level, it was relatively easy to see conceptual bonds between a poetry of love and a philosophy suffused with the idea of love.

The common denominator linking lyric poetry to abstract speculation was provided by the definition of love which constituted one of the prime tenets of Platonic doctrine. According to this definition, love was no more than the desire for beauty, goodness, and truth. It was inevitable that such a definition, and the philosophy behind it, would appeal to an age steeped in aestheticism and captivated by the notion of love. The first modern formulation of the Platonic theory of love was Marsilio Ficino's *Commentarium in Convivium Platonis de Amore* (1484), in which the author discussed such issues as the nature of love, its role in man's moral life, and its relation to the beautiful and the good. Although the work was of a metaphysical bent, it had serious repercussions on literature. "The Platonic *trattato d'amore* is a literary genre which began with Marsilio Ficino's commentary on the *Symposium* of Plato, and achieved great vogue in the sixteenth century. It frequently took dialogue form and was usually written in Italian rather than in Latin."[1] The love treatise, Platonic or not, was the first genre to be almost exclusively composed in the vernacular. The treatises used the Platonic definition of love as a starting point, attracted to the notion that love was the desire to beget the beautiful in the beautiful, which could then be enjoyed fully. The spread of Platonism led, on the one hand, to the philosophical investigation of beauty and, on the other, to the subtle analysis of the definition of love, particularly to clarify the distinctions between love and desire.[2] The responsibility for popularizing and marketing the platonically inspired treatises on love in the vernacular must be assigned to Pietro Bembo. His work *Gli Asolani*, published in 1505, led the way, becoming the model for the genre.

Gli Asolani is a dialogue, as are the *Prose della volgar lingua* and many of Plato's own works. The conversations take place at the palace of Caterina Cornaro, Venetian queen of Cyprus, on her estate at Asolo. During a three-day period, three young men present varying opinions on the nature and import of love, in the company of three young ladies, while a wedding celebration is going on. The dialogue includes three encounters of the group, during which three diverse aspects of love are discussed.[3] In the first conversation, love is presented as a source of suffering, anguish, bitterness, and injury; the second speaker takes the opposing view, for love is the source of all joy. During the third group encounter, the final debator advocates a middle course, distinguishing between good and evil love and thereby resolving the antithetical proposals of the first two spokesmen. The synthesis achieved is Platonic, for it distinguishes between love directed to earthly ends and celestial love, which employs the beauty of the beloved woman to transcend the material and enter the spiritual realm of divine perfection. Bembo explains that love must be directed to the better qualities inherent in one's lady in order for it to be good. Physical attractions thus become the ornaments of the soul more than of the body. As suggested in Ficino's deliberations on Plato, *Gli Asolani* emphasizes that only the most dignified corporeal properties— eyes, ears, and mind—could appreciate beauty; the other senses tend to the materialistic knowledge of the beloved, who is thereby loved improperly for the wrong reasons. The conclusion of Bembo's treatise on love is in keeping with the current trend to merge ancient philosophy with Christianity, Plato with the Church. Marsilio Ficino had already achieved a satisfactory synthesis in his *Theologia Platonica,* revealing a new conception of the unity and universality of thought, so that the ancient philosopher could enrich and clarify Christian doctrine. Ficino's publications expressed the dominant ideas and aspirations of Humanism, which accounts for their popularity and considerable influence. *Gli Asolani* achieves a similar goal on a less speculative and more literary plane, expressing the aspirations and ideals of the cultural elite of the Renaissance.

Philosophical depth and speculative originality are not characteristics of the Bembian dialogue. The courtly setting, replete with beautiful ladies, a reigning monarch, tasteful entertainments, and social amenities, recalls the many gardens of literary tradition, where elegant women and noble gentlemen assembled to debate questions of love. Philosophically, little of import is introduced by the three speakers, although they ably represent the diverse aspects of current opinion. As required by the material under scrutiny, the tone is serious but not dogmatic. The atmosphere is that of the salon or court, not that of the Humanist academy. Within the framework of the Platonic dialogue, Bembo introduces motifs derived from the Provençal poets, Dante, the Dolce Stil Nuovo, and Petrarca. Literature combines easily and naturally with philosophy, so that it is occasionally difficult to perceive where one ends and the other begins, so perfect is the fusion. The first discussion is emblematized in the Petrarchan motive of *amore amaro* ("bitter love"), the second speaker concludes with the oxymoron of *dolce tormento* ("sweet torture"), while the final treatment of the beloved is both Platonic and literary: the lady is viewed as an instrument in the attainment of eternal happiness (a theme proper to the Dolce Stil Nuovo and Petrarca) which is to be achieved through love, which is the desire for perfection and union with the ideal, namely God (in the Christian interpretation of Platonism), whereas earthly love is insufficient for the world and is but the shadow of the true, changeless universe of God (a Platonic note which is echoed in Petrarca's longings for spiritual perfection).[4] Even certain images were shared by both the philosophers and poets. For example, Marsilio Ficino had called beauty the divine splendor inherent in matter, declaring light to be God's likeness on earth. There is an obvious tie here with Petrarca's emphasis on light imagery, such as the choice of the sun as a symbol for either divinity or the guiding spirit of the beloved. In fact, as the critic Toffanin has noted, it is difficult to have even an approximate line of demarcation between the contents of the love treatises of the Cinquecento, bathed in Neo-Platonism, and the commentaries on Petrarchan poetry.

Bembo's *Asolani* served as a model for the numerous treatises on love and beauty published during the sixteenth century. Their success is a striking example of the power of the printed word to diffuse knowledge but also to dilute it. On the whole, these treatises were popular literature written for mass consumption, appealing to the taste of the general reading public, which was an elite group of cultured people in the Renaissance. Platonism raised love to an elevated sphere, detaching it from the regions of bestiality and placing it on a level with Christian idealism. It also consecrated the concept of the beautiful, making matter a harbinger of the eternal Beauty. "In Platonic philosophy love is defined in terms of beauty. Love is desire of beauty or desire of birth or reproduction in beauty. Since Platonic love theory involves a whole system of ethics, beauty is a key concept in the moral realm. By its association with truth and goodness, beauty is related to the gnosiological field as well."[5] But, in general, this new and popularized rendition of Platonism appealed to refined and aristocratic taste, as is apparent in the choice of settings for these treatises: salons, the homes of the nobility, villas, palaces, courts, and gardens.

Worldly backdrops inspire fashionable conversations and these love treatises are frequently encyclopedic catchalls of popular opinion and thought, borrowing from Christian doctrine, Humanism, Platonic philosophy, both the vernacular and classical literary traditions, and prevailing taste. The main topic of these dialogues was invariably love, its effects, characteristics, and psychology. The first of these modern treatises was Mario Equicola's *Libro di natura d'amore* (Venice, 1525), which provides an eclectic, encyclopedic history of love by tracing it through poetry and literature. The text also covers the mythological, spiritual, metaphysical, and astrological aspects of love, followed by a theoretical discussion of the matter bolstered by a great many quotations from celebrated authorities. A far more complex philosophical work, Leone Ebreo's *Dialoghi d'amore* were doctrinally faithful to Neo-Platonic thought. A very popular publication, Leone Ebreo's dialogues were first printed in Rome in 1535 but underwent eleven new editions between 1528 and 1587. The book is a series of dialogues between Sophia, the symbol of wisdom, and Filone on the subject of love. The *Dialoghi* are concerned with some of the same Platonic issues investigated by Bembo in *Gli Asolani,* particularly the rapport of desire with love. Filone and Sophia argue that love is not synonymous with desire but lives in the constant denial of possession for when possession was acquired, it would signify the end of desire, whose cessation would also terminate love. Therefore, unsatiated desire acts as an incentive to constant, unchanging love. A similar topic is broached in Tullia d'Aragona's treatise *De la infinità di amore* (Venice, 1547). According to Leone Ebreo, any love that generates desire can be considered of spiritual value; however, a love born of desire is inherently fallacious and doomed to destruction once that desire has been sated. A true spiritual love can survive the death of desire or elevate it.

The majority of these Renaissance tracts emphasize the notion of reciprocal transformation undergone by the lover who, through love, becomes the beloved and vice versa. The union thus achieved is decidedly spiritual, for, as even the courtesan Tullia notes, physical union can never permit the total penetration of the bodies and can therefore never satisfy the craving for union. The motif of the union of lovers is a *topos* in these disquisitions on love. Whereas Leone Ebreo had declared that two mutual lovers become one in their unity in love, or even four as each metamorphoses into the other and is both lover and beloved, successive treatise writers generally opted for a simpler transformation. Sperone Speroni, in his *Dialogo d'amore* (1542), felt that love unified the two, while Tullia d'Aragona preferred Leone's vision of four in one. In all cases, love treatises based on Platonic ideology stressed the need to ascend from the senses to the mind, positing a spiritual interpretation of love. The correlative concept of beauty also had to be justified by placing it on a ladder of all beauties, material and rational, leading to the perfect divine beauty. Love and beauty thereby become identified with goodness. The birth of love through the contemplation of beauty could then be justified on moral and spiritual grounds. Good love implied the recognition of the ideal hidden in the material and temporary, as well as the awareness of the presence of divinity in mortality. By correctly loving another human being, one loved God.

As part of their basic composition, the love tracts often presented a number of questions and issues to be debated and resolved. The interlocutors generally applied the deductive Socratic method of questions and answers, leading to a definitive response to the initial query. For example, in her dialogue Tullia d'Aragona asks if it is possible to love for a limited time (it is), while in Betussi's *Il Raverta* one of the speakers, found reading Leone Ebreo, is asked the exact definition of love, leading the participants to subdivide love into types and categories, only to arrive at Plato's conclusion that two kinds of love and two types of beauty exist. There are two Venuses, the sacred and the profane.

Not all the treatises on love were of a Platonizing disposition. One notable exception was Francesco Sansovino's *Ragionamento d'amore* (1545), the work he dedicated to Gaspara Stampa. The booklet retains the dialogue format but its topics are more earthbound than those of his contemporaries who devoted themselves to the genre. The interlocutors discuss such matters as: is it best to love a maiden, married woman, widow, or nun? what is the ideal age of a lover? do merchants, priests, soldiers, or noblemen make better lovers? The love so scrutinized is decidedly not Platonic. Another related development in the Renaissance's continuous and untiring affair with love was the academic lecture. The most famous of these scholarly disquisitions were Benedetto Varchi's *Lezzioni*, Sunday-afternoon lectures delivered to the Florentine Academy in the mid-1500s. Many of these lessons were devoted to literary criticism of Dante and Petrarca, but others considered the subject at hand: love. In June 1554, he presented the Academy with a discussion on the "Seven doubts concerning love," which included some Platonic topics, such as the question of whether the beautiful and the good were one and the same, or if all beautiful objects were good even if they were of a worldly nature. Other topics were less philosophical and included such questions as the embarrassment lovers feel in confessing their emotions or the necessity of returning any lover's love. Varchi presented a total of four lectures concerned with twenty-two such questions, all presumably of public interest given the educated and scholarly makeup of his audience.

The majority of treatise readers were not scholars but educated men and women who were drawn to the blend of Platonic theory, literary background, and society banter, very like the actual conversations taking place in the Italian salons of the Cinquecento. This tone rendered the subject matter enjoyable, easily digestible, and considerably watered down for the vast readership. The popularity of these works insured the diffusion of the information they contained. Soon the ideas of Plato, diluted and simplified, trickled into the mainstream of Renaissance life. Neo-Platonic concepts and vocabulary were integrated into the vocabulary and pattern of thought, becoming a natural part of any educated individual's linguistic and cultural environment. Even courtesans Platonized with the same superficial ease they demonstrated when Petrarchizing. Gaspara Stampa was doubtlessly associated with the circle of people who produced the treatises on love and was inevitably familiar with their contents and background sources. Acquainted with both Speroni and Varchi, Gaspara was on amicable terms with Francesco Sansovino, who had dedicated his *Ragionamento* to her as well as his edition of a Varchi lesson. Her brother Baldassare was not only an intimate friend of Sansovino, but was also mentioned in Betussi's *Il Raverta*. Betussi himself, the author of yet another treatise on love, *Leonora*, had been the private secretary of Collaltino di Collalto before becoming a professional writer. Even the celebrated courtesan Tullia d'Aragona had lived for some time in Venice, having as her intimate friend and consequently as a participant in her own Platonic dialogue the man of learning, Benedetto Varchi. Venetian high society was impregnated with the ideas and concepts propounded by the Platonizers and disciples of love. Plato, like Petrarca, was in the air, discussed, debated, read, misread, or merely inhaled.

Traces of Platonism blend into Gaspara Stampa's Petrarchismo effortlessly, as they did throughout the literary production of the sixteenth century. The *Rime* offer some of the philosopher's notions— filtered through the treatises and through Petrarca's own *Canzoniere*— not in speculative terms, but integrated into the fabric of Stampa's poetic themes and imagery. In a number of poems addressed to a certain Guiscardo, found among the "Rime Varie," Gaspara employs the Platonic theory of two types of love—spiritual and sensual—to explain the nature of their relationship. This Guiscardo was apparently a suitor inclined to do his wooing in verse. Stampa responds in kind, suggesting that she would allow his love, but only on a ultrasensual level. She appeals to his better qualities—honor, virtue, valor, and courtesy—by emphasizing her own treasured *onestade*. Having established the premises, she then makes a case for spiritual love, "any love born of these frail senses is brief, and oftentimes evil, for it slays the path we must take to heaven" (CCLXXX). The following sonnet reiterates the Platonic idiom as expressed in Leone Ebreo and Speroni when it speaks of ". . . that great love, which you show me, moves the lover and makes divided wills become one." Another echo of Leone Ebreo is heard in Stampa's definition of love, which is unlike desire: "It's very true that the desire with which I love you is full of honesty and love, anything else would be unfitting for us both" (CCLXXXII). Used in this fashion, the Platonic vocabulary has the function of gently rebuffing an ardent would-be lover, whom Stampa cannot or will not accept in real terms, while still acknowledging the value of his love by spiritualizing it. Platonic language has served to ward off flirtatious advances by making them innocuous through their very superiority. On the level of the quotidian, these sonnets to Guiscardo are rejections couched in the vocabulary of acceptance.

Neo-Platonism has profound thematic and imagistic influences on Stampa's love poetry, which supersede the sophisticated gallantry of the sonnets to Guiscardo. The idealization of Collaltino into a poetic *persona* independent of his ontological self is realized by borrowing from both the Petrarchan traditions and Platonic ideas. The historical Collaltino di Collalto, Count of Treviso, is not the actual subject of Gaspara's poetry. The beloved is the man artistically called *conte* and *signore* but never *Collaltino*. Stampa's encounter poem "Era vicino il

dì" (II), discussed in the previous chapter of this book, is an
illustration of the fusion of Platonic and Petrarchan elements in the
Rime and an example of the ideal representation of the beloved.
Certain images are typical of an anniversary sonnet: the choice of
Christmas day; the parallel drawn between the beloved and Christ, the
lover and Mary; the religious and personal symbolism of the feast
day; the ensuing contrast between the poetic *persona*'s inner state and
the external manifestations of the holiday. Stampa's correlation of the
human and the divine, however, is not derived directly from Petrarca,
who reveres Laura but never associates her with God or the Virgin.
Stampa clearly fuses Christ and the beloved and parallels her own
acceptance of her lord's love to the Annunciation in a manner which
might be sacrilegious were it not Platonic. According to doctrine, love
is the force which binds inferior and superior worlds in a union; in
poetic terms, there are two levels of superiority and inferiority at work
in the sonnet. On the first, she is subservient to her *signore* ("lord" or
"Lord"), who deigns to love her, just as Mary, a human, was
acquiescent to the will of the divine Creator; on the second level, the
love for a mortal becomes only a phase in the love for God. Desiring
his human perfections inevitably leads her to the desire for total
perfection. Just as Mary's love for God, incarnated in Christ, leads to
the ascension of all humanity, Gaspara's love leads her upward. This
interpretation is substantiated by a birth metaphor from Leone Ebreo's
Dialoghi: the beloved is the father, the lover is the mother who bears
love, the child. An inevitable consequence of this symbolism is the
association of human and divine love, as this diagram helps illustrate:

$$Gaspara = mother = Mary = lover$$
$$signore = father = God = beloved$$
$$human\ love = child = Christ = love\ (human\ and\ divine)$$

The merging of Platonism and Petrarchismo is essential to the understanding of Stampa's *signore*. The multiple meaning of the word
takes on particular significance where he is concerned, for he is
concurrently a master in the feudal sense, a gentleman, a superior
being in the tradition of courtly literature, and a god. Occasionally, all
these aspects unite:

> Chi vuol veder l'imagin del valore,
> l'albergo de la vera cortesia,
> il nido di bellezza e leggiadria,
> la stanza de la gloria alta e d'onore,
> venga a veder l'illustre mio signore,
> dove si trova ciò che si disia,
> fino il mio cor e fino l'alma mia,
> chi gli diè già, né poi mi rese, Amore. (CXXI)

(Whoever wants to see the image of valor, the abode of true kind courtesy, the nest of beauty and grace, the quarters of great glory and honor, come see my illustrious lord, where you can find whatever you desire, even my heart and my soul as well, that Love gave him and never returned to me.)

Stampa does not present a Venus or an effeminate male variation of the goddess of Love but a Mars, as perfect as any god in all his deeds, demeanor, virility, strength, and appearance. He indeed houses all the principal masculine attributes, but they remain vague because of the very essence of his perfection. Even his physical characteristics are general. In poem VII, Gaspara informs her audience that he possesses a "sweet" and *"vago"* mien, which implies ineffable grace and undefinable beauty in the Petrarchan lexicon, while his hair is blond— like Laura's—and his chest broad. Nothing is specific: gods and icons do not possess crooked noses or buck teeth. Like other "images," the beloved exists in a superior sphere, indifferent to the matters of mere mortals. As distant as any unsmiling Aztec deity, this "lord" receives the sacrifices of his faithful, the "heart and soul" of the lover. Having thus lost her identity, the lover has fused into the beloved, no longer belonging to herself. The beloved's responsibilities are unclear, however. Some Neo-Platonists maintained that, being in possession of the lover, it naturally followed that love must be reciprocal, since the beloved does no more than love a part of himself by returning the love given by the lover. But this illustrious lord appears only to receive amorous tributes. The poetic Collaltino is narcissistic, a lover of self alone, enamoured of his own beauty: "have pity and turn your gaze now and then from your beauties to my pain" (XXII).

Beauty is an integral part in this process of deification of the beloved, who is constantly detached from the real human world in both body and soul. As Stampa declares time and again, his is a "divine, not human beloved countenance" (XII). "Gaspara Stampa's Neoplatonism comes to the fore, where the lover, even in corporeal form and through his active virtues, is the translucent reflection, the resplendent image, or, to use Plotinian terminology, the emanation descended into matter of the fullness and perfection of the ideal world, the Truth, the static and eternal One."[6] In the Platonic terms then popular, material beauty should be loved since it causes the knowledge and love of perfect immaterial beauty. To this, Bembo added in *Gli Asolani* that beauty was a proportion and a harmony. The more perfect these were, the more worthy the beautiful object was of love. The vague, undefined features of the count, their proportionate nature, and his attractive generalities are a sign, the external manifestation of the beloved's inner worth. His unspecified outer pulchritude is the ideal expression of spiritual harmony. He transfigures human reality, sanctifying the natural by infusing it with the metaphysical. Collaltino thus becomes the undescribably perfect product of creation, "the most beautiful creature ever made by the prime cure (God)" (LV). A perfect creature, he is venerated, idolized, and celebráted through her love. Although love is the desire for both physical (known through the senses) and incorporeal (known through reason and the mind) beauty, it is generally love for the count's unquestionable charms and attributes which holds and attracts Gaspara to him. She can aspire to rational love only when the flesh is no longer present.

But this corporeal love is expressed through Platonic idealization. The appeal of infinity is lodged in one human form. And while Stampa cannot generally sublimate her all too human emotion to the point of viewing her love as the means of achieving spiritual ascension, she does create a sublime substitute for God, another type of elevated truth and good and beauty to which she can aspire: art. In many Stampian poems, loving becomes not the way to spiritual ascent but the *modus operandi* to artistic expression. Love is transfigured into poetry. Art replaces the religious experience associated with Christian Neo-Platonism. Love provides a ladder, not to God, but to self-completion and fulfillment in the sphere of art. Human beauty engenders poetic beauty: "If it happen that I write or speak, narrating my loving labor, it is not I, nay, but your lovely beautiful eyes" (LXXIV). The upward thrust of Platonism, moving from the reflecting object to the ideal, goes from perfect man to the realm of art in the poetry of Gaspara Stampa.

Just as the lover cannot extricate herself from the love for her lord's corporeal beauty, the count is also inextricably woven into the fabric of the material world. Nor is this contrary to the tenets and habits of Renassance Neo-Platonism. As Luigi Russo has pointed out,[7] the period's Platonism is immersed in matter and bound to the physical. Love and beauty are given corporeal shape. Ideas are expressed in similes and metaphors derived from the natural universe, rather than in metaphysical imagery. It is logical for Stampa to compare her beloved with the manifestations of the external world. A significant example is sonnet IV of the *Rime*, where the qualities of her beloved are compared to the planetary bodies: from Saturn he received intelligence; Jupiter taught him to seek beauty and worthiness; Mars granted bellicosity, Apollo artistry, Mercury eloquence, Venus beauty and charm, while the moon "made him a bit colder than I would like." In the fifth poem of the volume, Stampa likens him to the heavenly bodies, the elements, and the seasons:

> Io assomiglio il mio signor al cielo
> meco sovente. Il suo bel viso è 'l sole;
> gli occhi, le stelle; e 'l suon de le parole
> è l'armonia, che fa 'l signor di Delo.
>   Le tempeste, le piogge, i tuoni e 'l gelo
> son i suoi sdegni, quando irar si suole;
> le bonacce e 'l sereno è quando vuole
> squarciar de l'ire sue benigno il velo.
>   La primavera e 'l germogliar de' fiori
> è quando ei fa fiorir la mia speranza,
> promettendo tenermi in questo stato.
>   L'orrido verno è poi, quando cangiato
> minaccia di mutar pensieri e stanza,
> spogliata me de' miei più ricchi onori. (V)

(I often liken my lord to the heavens. His beautiful face is the sun; his eyes, the stars, and the sound of his voice is the harmony made by Delos' lord. The tempests, rains, thunder, and ice are his rage when he's wont to anger; the lulls and calm are when he benignly wants to dispel the veil of anger. Spring and the budding flowers are when he makes my hopes flower, promising to keep me in this state. Horrid winter comes when he's transformed and menaces to change both mind and residence, stripping me of my richest honors.)

Thus, the idea of the beloved's power, superiority, and mutability is materialized in the forces of nature which control men's lives: the life-giving sun, the astrological stars, climate, and seasonal change.

In Italian poetic tradition, the exaltation of the beloved can reach hyperbolic levels, as seen in Petrarca and the poets of the Dolce Stil Nuovo, where the lady is attributed magical and/or mystical powers. Stampa's own count is compared to a wizard, a Medusian figure who can transform reality through the mere strength of his gaze. His is the mesmerizing quality of the enchanter who subdues all; his "fatal eyes" could make animals, grass, plants, water, winds, women, and even stones "burn with love" (XX). Similar phantasmagoric powers are given to his singing. Like the mythic hero, Orpheus, he can quiet storms, sweeten all ills, and pacify nature, taming even lions and tigers (XXXI). Like Orpheus, Collaltino is also possessed of the power over life and death where Gaspara—Eurydice—is concerned. He is lord and master, lifegiver and creator; she is his "prisoner" and "making," with no redeeming qualities. She denigrates self to elevate him, offering herself as incense at the altar of her idol. A symbol of this new god are his eyes, capable of subtracting the rays from the sun, the weapons from Amor, and beauty from Venus herself (CXVIII). In philosophical terms, light is associated with the Platonic good; it is through the eyes that beauty is perceived and thus known and the eyes, in the Petrarchan idiom, are mirrors of the soul and, thereby, of God. Using literary tradition, Neoplatonic concepts, and her own imagery, Stampa creates a new marvel, an ideal man so wondrous as to be celestial, not earthly.

The sacrifice for love is a religious immolation, the pagan worship of a human deity. This surrender to a superior being is described in the vocabulary of Neo-Platonism and the love tracts: in a mystic exchange of identities, the two become one, or four, as expressed in this Stampian madrigal:

> Così m'impresse al core
> la beltà vostra Amor co' raggi suoi,
> che di me fuor mi trasse e pose in voi;
> or che son voi fatt'io,
> voi meco una medesma cosa séte,
> onde al ben, al mal mio,
> come al vostro, pensar sempre devete. (CCXXIII)

(Love thus engraved your beauty in my heart with his rays, drawing me from myself and placing me in you; now that I've become you, you are one thing with me, so that you must always think about my joys and ills, which are your own.)

The desire to acquire beauty through union with the beloved in the most perfect manner conceivable permits a subtle distinction between spiritual transformation and physical possession. It is a distinction Stampa and many of her contemporaries did not make. In the Petrarchan model, Laura was neither attained nor attainable; the suffering lover was doomed to perpetual frustration. The Renaissance accepted the natural as well as the transcendent character of love. The fulfillment sought by Gaspara included physical union and sensual desire, which were acknowledged as constituent parts of love by many. Even within the confines of her limited Neo-Platonism, Stampa understood love as composed of both physical and spiritual elements that were not in conflict: "Oh, Love, you are quite wicked and quite unjust to suffer that lovers be so far apart from each other in body and in heart!" (LXII).

The lack of love is also depicted through a variation on a Platonic theme. In his tract *On Love*, Marsilio Ficino had written: "Without a doubt there are two species of Love; one is simple, the other mutual. Simple Love occurs when the Beloved does not love the Lover. Therefore, the Lover is totally dead, because he does not live in himself, . . . and does not live in the Beloved, being scorned by him/ her."[8] This death in self is a consequence of the exchange of identities which takes place in love; if love is unrequited, the person who does love loses his identity to the other. Stampa proposes this "miracle" of love in poetic terms: "Sir, I know that I no longer live in myself, and now I see that I am also dead in you . . . it can be said that my true essence . . . is the image of Echo and of Chimera" (CXXIV). The dissolution of self is represented in Platonic terminology and through a mythical metaphor. In one version of the Greek myth, the nymph Echo had wasted away for love of Narcissus (Collaltino?), who could only love himself; what remained was a voice. Stampa also retains her voice, which is revived in the words of her poetry, itself an echo of other voices and past poems, all of which are echoes of Love's inspiration. As for the Chimera, she is a dream creature with no roots in reality, a creation of the mind, and a mirror of other beings—the Chimera is formed of lion, goat, and dragon—with no true identity. She is like Stampa the poetic *persona*, who has molded herself into a mirror for her beloved, losing her identity by entering his, only to be annihilated in his rejection.

The theme of the division of self is repeated often in the *Rime*, generally in images of life and death, or in certain poetic metaphors, such as that of the double heart which the beloved holds since he is in possession of both his own and hers (LV, CCXXVIII), or that of the soulless self, "for I am really living without a soul or heart in my bosom" (LVI). Related to this Platonic loss of identity through love, jealousy is a novel theme undertaken by Stampa and a few other *cinquecentisti*. Arguing with Amor, Gaspara asks what has happened to her for having given her soul and heart to her lord: "how can it be . . . that I feel cold jealousy and misgiving, and that I am deprived of all gaiety and joy, if I live in him, and live without myself in me?" (CXXXII). The *persona* never accomplishes the miracle augured by Amor. Although she dies to herself, she is not reborn in him. Next to the luminous—and Platonically so—image of the beloved, she is depicted as darkness, life contrasting with death, happiness with pain. She is first introduced as the "image of death and martyrdom" (VII), accompanied by tears and sighs. Love in the Stampian *canzoniere* feeds on death, pain, and jealousy. Joy itself is mingled with suffering. Life-giving love is related to death and understood in terms of loss, both of self and of one's individuality. Without him, she is undefined, in an emotional and personal limbo, "because this way I don't know what I am" (LXXXIV).

It is only with separation and after abandon that Stampa can completely sublimate her love, detaching it from any ties with matter and relegating it to the ideal world. Once the beloved is gone, leaving the unrequited lover, the corporeal man and his spiritual image are severed, allowing the continuation of love without the need for physical contact or reciprocity, in the state Ficino termed "Simple Love." In the final poems of the *Rime* dedicated to him, Collaltino becomes an essence, a totally incorporeal creature, to be loved through the mind and spirit rather than through the senses and the flesh. He thus becomes two beings: his actual physical self and the object of her ethereal affections.

The terrain for this poetic transformation into an immaterial being had already been prepared in the Platonic terminology of some of the earlier sonnets:

> Voi potete, signor, ben tôrmi voi
> con quel cor d'indurato diamante,
> e farvi d'altra donna novo amante;
> di che cosa non è, che più m'annoi;
>   ma non potete già ritôrmi poi
> l'imagin vostra, il vostro almo sembiante,
> che giorno e notte mi sta sempre innante,
> poi che mi fece Amor de' servi suoi. (CLXXI)

(You could, lord, take yourself away from me with that heart of yours, as hard as any diamond, and become another woman's brand-new lover: though nothing would pain me more! But you can never take away your image, your immortal countenance, that stands before me all day and night since Love made a slave of me.)

Having previously presented the possibility of an immortal image to replace the actual beloved, Stampa could infuse the last sonnets to her first love with Platonic suggestions and concepts without destroying the unity of her *canzoniere*. Her individual "sun" is converted into a stepping stone to the "great Sun" God; the Petrarchan metaphor of the boat at sea is used, as it was originally intended, to depict the spiritual voyage to the Almighty. Having lost hope of ever seeing "those serene lights" of her beloved again, Stampa chooses the eternal light and "without fear of hitting rocks, I live in a quiet and secure harbor" (CCII). Soon thereafter, she repudiates external beauty in favor of the soul, replacing the nourishment of the senses with "a better food to feed the mind," thus tempering her "hot-blooded and blind love, guided only by darkness and error" (CCIV). The mind and reason have replaced sensation and emotion as the only true means of understanding love and beauty.

The idol has lost its contours and become idea, abstraction, thought, and spirit. The true has replaced the false; beauty of mind has vanquished the mendacious and ephemeral beauties of the flesh. The idol survives, but the worshiper has come to deny not her deity, but his transient attributes. The sublimation of the count is completed. Made celestial image, he has become "that eternal and unmatched beauty, that does not rise or fall by chance, and cares not about time or others" (CCV). The beauty that inspired love and, consequently, poetry has been sanctified in his "true virtues":

> Canta tu, musa mia, non più quel volto,
> non più quegli occhi e quell'alme bellezze,
> che 'l senso mal accorto par che prezze,
> in quest'ombre terrene impresso e involto;
>   ma l'alto senno in saggio petto accolto,
> mille tesori e mille altre vaghezze
> del conte mio, e tante sue grandezze,
> ond'oggi il pregio a tutti gli altri ha tolto. (CCVI)

(Muse, sing that face no more, nor those eyes and immortal beauties that unwise sense, inscribed and enveloped in these earthly shades, appears to prize; sing the noble wisdom gathered in a sage breast, a thousand treasures and a thousand other charms belonging to my count, and his many great qualities, with which he's won the praise from one and all.)

And it is with this virtuous deity, this god become idea, that the love poems to Collaltino end. The spiritual apotheosis is complete.

Chapter Five
A Poet for All Time

"I Feel My Heart Engraved with a New Style" (VIII)

Neither a consummate *petrarchista* nor a genuine Platonist, Gaspara Stampa left her unique mark on the lyric poetry of the Cinquecento and on all Italian literature. Today she is considered one of the best, if not the best, poets of her century. She was, without a doubt, one of the most significant women writers ever to appear in the history of Italian letters. Her originality stems not from a rebellion against the accepted literary conventions of her day or from a denial of tradition but from her ability to integrate both convention and tradition into her personal poetic idiom. Working in a highly structured and formalized genre, Stampa unavoidably elected to employ established patterns and to adhere to set standards, often accommodating her diction and themes to conventional molds. While outwardly traditional and rich in Petrarchan traces, the *Rime* offer a discriminating reader a unique and varied harmony of tones.

One source of this poetic consistency is the everyday quality of much of Stampa's language and content, which caused so many critics to judge it a diary, confession, or epistolary in verse. The quotidian pervades this collection of apparently imitative poetry, translating into a prosaic linguistic quality. Common speech intrudes into the territory of the purified, even rarified, aulic tongue proposed by the *bembisti*. The value of Stampa's poetry lay in its rejection of the rhetorical experiences of her contemporaries; she had instinctively chosen an immediate mode of expression in a century unused to immediacy and generally concerned with the propagation of the Petrarchan myth and the reproduction of the poet's paradigmatic vicissitudes.[1] Gaspara's literary vocabulary moves toward the spoken rather than the formal written tongue, resulting in an aura of directness and sincerity lacking in her more polished contemporaries, who either possessed a better grasp of traditional prosody or were more concerned with the Ciceronian poetics of *gravitas* so often espoused by the intelligentsia. To achieve this incursion into the quotidian, Stampa employed a variety of techniques: direct address, direct discourse in soliloquies and dialogues between poetic *personae,* and indirect discourse as a substitute for immediate conversation.

The figure of Amor is especially loquacious throughout the *Rime,* holding long conversations in verse with the protagonist. Other entities and beings, however, also "speak" to the lover. In poem LIII, an unknown fear in her heart announces the possible loss of the count's love, while in LXXXVII an impersonal subject says of her, " 'This woman burns and wastes away in vain for someone.' " The poet even quotes directly from the beloved's messages, alternating his words with those of others: "Sometimes I trust in my darling's letters, sometimes I despair at someone's words; he tells me, ' I will come'; someone says, 'He won't' " (XCII). On occasion, Stampa quotes the count's spoken, rather than written, words, resulting in some commonplace and prosaic lines which capture the modulations of colloquial speech. Only the rhyme scheme of this tercet distinguishes it from prose: "—Io ti scriverò subito—mi dite—/ch'io sarò giunto al loco ove andar chero;—/e poi la vostra fede a me tradite" (" 'I'll write as soon,' you tell me, 'as I arrive at the place where I must go.' And then you betray my trust in you") (CXXXVI). The poet even quotes herself as her own protagonist, enacting short plays in sonnet form, like her dialogue with Amor in CXXXII. In some compositions, she addresses her afflicted soul, while in CCI the *persona* of Anassilla chides her beloved for his indifference. One poem offers a fascinating plunge into the modernistic region of the interior monologue. The speaker is talking to herself; her soliloquy is essentially a reverie, for she is daydreaming about her distant beloved:

> —Or sopra il forte e veloce destriero—
> io dico meco—segue lepre o cerva
> il mio bel sole, or rapida caterva
> d'uccelli con falconi o con sparviero.
> Or assal con lo spiedo il cignal fiero,

quando animoso il suo venir osserva;
or a l'opre di Marte, or di Minerva
rivolge l'alto e saggio suo pensiero.
   Or mangia, or dorme, or leva ed or ragiona,
or vagheggia il suo colle, or con l'umana
sua maniera trattiene ogni persona.—
   Così, signor, bench'io vi sia lontana,
sí fattamente Amor mi punge e sprona,
ch'ogni vostr'opra m'è presente e piana. (CXLVII)

("Now on his strong and swift steed," I tell myself, "my beautiful
sun pursues hares and stags, or a quick flock of birds with falcons
and sparrowhawks. Now he attacks a fierce boar with his spear,
having boldly observed his approach; now he turns his noble and
wise thoughts to Mars' or Minerva's deeds. Now he eats, now he
sleeps, now he's up, and now he speaks, now he fondly gazes upon
his hill, and now in his gracious way, he entertains one and all."
Sir, as you can see, although I'm far from you, Love wounds and
urges me on in such a way that your every deed is present and clear
to me.)

The sonnet is creative not only because of the original employment of
a modified type of stream of consciousness, that is, the description of
the *persona*'s current of thought as it unfolds, but also due to the
complexity of the communication. The poem is structured, in itself, as
a message to her *signor,* but within this first level of address there
exists a second addressee, the poet-protagonist herself. This second
dialogue is presented in a separate syntactical frame: direct discourse.
There exist two recipients of the same message, the poet and the count.
Interior monologue and external dialogue are thus merged in the same
poetic structure.

Related to her employment of direct and indirect discourse, Stampa
also makes considerable use of apostrophe, invocation and address,
directed to herself, her poetry, the Muses, an undefined audience of
women or readers, the hills and rivers of Collaltino's domains, Love,
Venus, various artists, her literary friends and acquaintances, and,
most often, the beloved. The reader naturally and inevitably views
himself as the other participant in this poetic dialogue, assuming the

role of count, Amor, Venus, or the generic *donne* for the duration of the poem. Stampa thus subtly involves her audience in the statements of her verse, creating a silent partner in her literary conversations. Of course, all poetry seeks to communicate, but Stampa's repeated engagement of a declared second presence deepens this already existing rapport between reader and poet. The simplicity and spontaneity of some of Stampa's language favor the development of such a relationship. Free of much of the polished rhetoric of her time, Stampa's *Rime* marry colloquialism to conventionality. Some lines of verse read like descriptive or narrative prose, with none of the elegant refinements of Petrarchan or Bembian poetry and imitations. But they are full of the immediacy of daily life and real emotion. Often, this Stampian simplicity is appended to otherwise artificial or imitative compositions. A specific instance is poem CXXXIII, which abounds in complex rhetorical devices such as antithesis, oxymoron, play on words, and anaphora. A rather artificial work based on the Platonic notion of death in life ("without having life, I live in pain") Stampa's sonnet is an able linguistic variation on this theme, until the final dramatic tercet which is effective because of the very contrast presented with the rest of the work. Its language is simple and unadorned and, thereby, authentic and moving: "What ends Love and heaven have in store for me I do not know, alas, nor could I say; I know full well that I'm in an unhappy way."

Some of Stampa's superior poetry is achieved when her linguistic spontaneity meets an appropriate theme or suits an emotional state. This simple and expressive language is at its best when used to present concrete images or natural snatches of everyday life, unspoiled by the poet's employment of rhetorical devices, which seem to blend imperceptibly into the fabric of the work. The poems heralding Collaltino's return from France are indicative of this Stampian manner, exuding the enthusiastic joy of expectancy, nervous hope, and loving vigil. Here, the fusion of technique, colloquial tone, emotional experience, and imagery has the ring of artistic truth, of feeling lived through poetry. Style comes to complement content. For example, the first of these four sonnets makes use of iteration, with the repetition of the interjection "o," to express wonder, joy, surprise, and merriment. The final tercet heightens this emotional "high," through the employment of a series of three rhetorical questions, which makes vocal and mental inflection rise, in a crescendo which is both linguistic and affecting, doing justice to the *persona*'s condition of joy and elation (C). The following sonnet is less excited emotionally and semantically, but equally joyous in a tender, intimate fashion. Once again, the conventions of Petrarchan poetry are used to complement the subject matter:

> Con quai degne accoglienze o quai parole
> raccorrò io il mio gradito amante,
> che torna a me con tante glorie e tante,
> quante in un sol non vide forse il sole?
> Qual color or di rose, or di viole
> fia 'l mio? qual cor or saldo ed or tremante,
> condotta innanzi a quel divin sembiante,
> ch'ardir e tèma insieme dar mi suole?
> Osarò io con queste fide braccia
> cingerli il caro collo, ed accostare
> 'la mia tremante a la sua viva faccia?
> Lassa, che pur a tanto ben penare
> temo che 'l cor di gioia non si sfaccia:
> chi l'ha provato se lo può pensare. (CI)

(With what worthy welcomes and with what words will I receive my welcome lover, who returns to me with so very many honors, that even the sun has never seen so many in one man? Will the color of roses or of violets be mine? will my heart be steady or trembling as I'm led before that divine countenance, which is wont to grant me temerity and fear together? Will I dare embrace his dear neck with these faithful arms, and approach my trembling face to his animated one? Weary me, although I suffer for such good, I fear my heart will dissolve in its joy: whoever has known it can well imagine how.)

Here too, the syntax serves a thematic function. The interrogatives reflect the feeling of happy uncertainty, as do the sequences of antithesis (steady-trembling, temerity-fear, suffering-joy), and certain sound patterns and repetitions (e.g., *torna . . . tante . . . tante . . . quante*). Certain Renaissance *topoi* also appear: he is the "divine countenance" associated with his apotheosis; the sun represents both

the planetary body, life, and the divinity (there is also the play on
words and equivocal internal rhyme formed by *sol*, "alone" or "only,"
and *sole*, "sun"); and the presence of interjectory expressions (*lassa*)
typical of the Petrarchan school. Many of the themes are singularly
Stampian, however: the sense of loss of the self in love, the coexistence
of happiness and pain, expressed in terms of dissolution, and the
protestations of fidelity. On the whole, the language is spontaneous
and colloquial, having the rhythm of common speech. The images
depicted in the first tercet are both original, natural, and tenderly
feminine, as the protagonist fantasizes their reunion in physical but
not erotic terms, ending in a concrete but symbolic gesture of love.
Even the final general remark made in the fourteenth line is exemplary
in its prosaic vagueness: she can say no more, but anyone who has
loved has shared her feelings; let the reader fill in the rest.

The two remaining sonnets of this series dedicated to the beloved's
return share the linguistic, stylistic, and thematic unity of the first. CII
employs the conventional sun metaphor and the Petrarchan antithesis
of war-peace to symbolize the coming of joy and the departure of pain.
The frenzied state of rapt expectancy of happiness is semantically
rendered through the use of the independent subjunctive to express a
wish or desire, very similar in tone to an exclamation: "Let darkness
and clouds be gone from me," "Let everything in me be filled with
laughter," "Let my life be enveloped in a thousand sweet chosen
pleasures." CIII is Stampa's benedicite to love, "Io benedico, Amor,"
composed on a series of anaphora, parallel constructions, and Petrar-
chan-Platonic images of light—nothing less than a paean to his return.
Nor is this successful fusion of style and content limited to these
sonnets. Often realistic images reflective of everyday life and emotions
are joined to knowledgeable use of language and rhetorical devices.
Sentiments which would be considered plebeian and trite by many of
her contemporaries appear in Stampa's poetry, such as worry. In one
poem of separation, Gaspara expresses a maternal preoccupation that
"some misfortune has befallen him" and the more passionate appre-
hension that "he only thinks on me when I am near, while absence
separates his heart from me" (XCIX). In another composition,
inspired by the conventional image of the guiding eyes, the poet
concludes with a palpably human picture drawn from real experience:

"alas, poor me, why doesn't he knock at my doors?" (XLIX). In a line, Stampa has swept away the artificiality of the Petrarchan metaphor and introduced the world of actuality, the feel and touch of day-to-day life. Nor is the poet above capitalizing on platitudes and clichés in her prosaism, borrowing readily from the colloquial vocabulary of her time.

Stampian prosody is also unique for its musical qualities. The tuneful properties of some compositions can be attributed to her status as a *virtuosa*. Since the poet was an expert musician and singer, trained in the setting of poetry to music, it is not surprising that many of her works are extremely melodious and distinguished by their gracefulness, rhythm, and sound patterns, rather than their contents. The words convey meaning through tone, echo, rhyme, resonance, and modulation. The cadence of the madrigals is particularly suggestive. Words lose their individual denotative role and create connotative sound patterns, thus ceasing much of their lexical significance and becoming musical notes in the poetic composition:

> Qual fosse il mio martìre
> nel vostro dipartire,
> voi 'l potete di qui, signor, stimare,
> che mi fu tolto infin il lagrimare. (CCXXIX)

(What my martyrdom was like when you departed, sir, can be judged by the fact that even weeping has been denied me.)

The simplicity of meaning of such poems, joined to their catchy tunefulness, shows Stampa to be a precursor of the Arcadian school of poetry which flourished in the eighteenth century, as well as of melic poetry and the Metastasian melodrama, alongside the sweet and limpid *canzonette* that were so popular in the Settecento. At times, Stampa possesses the languor and pathos proper to the melodrama or the simplicity of diction and content belonging to the new pastoral school. Her harmony offers "neither power, drama, complexity, nor vehement and deep music, but a facile and felicitous streak, capable of a light design in which spontaneous and lively feelings are released in a limpid melodramatic song."[2] The recall of the Arcadia and Metastasio is apropos, for, like Gaspara, they did not seek to achieve a rhetorical type of poetry, but expressive purity, authentic emotion, and melody.

Gaspara Stampa's lyric idiom has a distinct identity, a private language of its own which is an amalgam of conventional style and themes, colloquial speech patterns, a mellifluous musical cadence, and an overall atmosphere of sincerity and spontaneity. She often joins tradition to everyday life, thus altering both. This stylistic transformation is representative of an individual interpretation of her own reality and, therefore, of an independent sensitivity, although both are participant in the taste and tradition of her age. There are elements of the epistolary, the confession, and the diary in Stampa's poetry, but these are purified and universalized by the very act of writing and the process of selection necessary to any artistic creation. Stampa's poetry is not life but its artistic translation. Her ability to fuse her personal reality and poetry is perhaps her greatest asset but it is also the origin of her major stylistic defects. The instruments of expression available are inevitably those recognized by social taste, sanctified by tradition, and accepted by the literary connoisseurs. At no time was this truer than in the sixteenth century. The uneven tones of Stampa's poetry derive from the alternation between spontaneity and imitation, originality and compliance. Stampa's tones are often uneven, occasionally trite, and sometimes insignificant. Caught between convention and instinctive talent, the poet totters in uncertainty. In many of her compositions, a single quatrain or tercet, or even a solitary line, shines with unique individuality, novelty, or daring, only to be smothered in its commonplace surroundings.

A justly famous example of this stylistic heterogeneity is poem XCI which initiates in typically Petrarchan fashion with praises of the beloved and love, "new and rare miracle of nature," only to undergo a literary metamorphosis. Stampa turns the tables on tradition, by placing herself above the lover, in a position of superiority justified by her exceptional faithfulness. The Petrarchan *topos* is thus overturned, the *dominus* no longer dominates but is supplanted by the supposedly inferior devotee. The true miracle of love is the awareness of the power of loving and sacrificing. Pain and loyalty give victory. The tercets are the *persona*'s cry of triumph. It is also a cry of defiance against those who do not understand the power of love to elevate and transcend human nature. Donadoni termed the final line "titanic" and it is a definite statement of the ascendancy of the lover over all. Unfortunately, these forceful tercets are preceded by some ordinary imitative quatrains, giving the entire composition an ambiguous character and unbalanced style:

> Quant'ei tutt'altri cavalieri eccede
> in esser bello, nobile ed ardito,
> tanto è vinto da me, da la mia fede.
> Miracol fuor d'amor mai non udito!
> Dolor, che chi nol prova non lo crede!
> Lassa, ch'io sola vinco l'infinito! (XCI)

(As he exceeds all other knights in beauty, dignity, and daring, so is he vanquished by me and my faith. Unheard of miracle except in love! Pain, unbelievable if untried! Weary though I be, only I conquer infinity!)

Original Themes and Personal Variations

Love in all its multiplicity, victories, defeats, fears, and fulfillments is the central theme and subject of Gaspara Stampa's poetry. This *canzoniere* is the personal history of the poet's dealings with love, more than with a lover or lovers. The beloved is only the efficient cause; love is the prime mover, which looms larger than any man or woman, no matter how divine, dominating everyone and everything with its omnipotence and ubiquity. It is this passion, more than the person of the beloved, that gives thematic cohesion to the "Rime d'Amore." It is with open arms and uncontested willingness that the feminine protagonist welcomes its overpowering presence.

Stampa's depiction of love lacks the consummate artistry or psychological subtlety of Petrarca's poetry, but it does contain a broader spectrum of emotions. Petrarca's *Canzoniere* was limited to a restricted gamut of sensations and responses, owing principally to its constant distancing of lover and beloved. Laura was an admired ideal, a creature of the imagination and the intellect as well as of the heart, kept forever unattainable and forever honored. The lover gazed upon his lady, but he never touched or possessed her. In the words of

Francesco De Sanctis, the great nineteenth-century literary critic, this love "is the first page of a novel, but we lack the novel or the story." In the Renaissance, this sacred distance was often canceled. Although in Platonic terms sight and hearing—the most perfect of the senses— were still hallowed by tradition, the other earthier faculties were not excluded from a fundamentally Petrarchan rapport in verse. Stampa's love poetry includes all aspects of a love relationship in all their gradations. Idealization gives way to denunciation, worship to re-proach, joy to jealousy, fulfillment to abandon. Feelings, in all their polychromatic possibilities, emerge from the pages of the *Rime,* giving it substance and the ring of psychological truth. Stampa appears as her own central character, a woman of complex and fascinating facets. Contradictions abound, but are reconciled through the unifying force of love, that inspires them all. "Her follies, doubts, weaknesses, ravings, that mixture of heroism and sublime pettiness, have the power of a confession. . . . Because her psychology is less controlled, but spontaneous and unreasoning, closer to desire, than was the bittersweet melancholy of Petrarca, with its prevailing calm and sorrowful tone, it frees itself with its fervor and passionate outbursts, which memory and regret cannot dissipate."[3]

Psychological awareness and frank expression are the great qualities of Stampa's work. Her personality as an artist, a woman, and a lover emerges even in the midst of some mediocre poetry, sloppy diction, and evident imitation. The reader is drawn to her inner drama, the conflicts and episodes of her literary love, and her sincerity. Stampa's lyricism issues from the torments and workings of her being and from her personal intuitions, with such concreteness as to be new, even when compared with the Petrarchan model. Her love blazes in its very fullness, less elevated than the master's, but more carnal and, therefore, more human. Senses and ideals merge. Stampa has a sensual honesty that acknowledges the traditional idiom of Petrarchismo and Neo-Platonism and imitates their vocabulary, while differentiating her own position. Using conventional terminology, she creates a sensuous atmosphere in her poetry which is pervasive but far from erotic, titillating, or pornographic. Even the most candid poems subsist in a rarefied atmosphere, free of any sexual or voluptuous detail. The famous—or infamous, according to certain Victorian critics—sonnet,

"O notte, a me più chiara," is suspended in verbal generalities. This precious night of love is described in a terminology suited for any, even the most spiritualized, chaste purpose. The adjectives employed to modify this night are inoffensive in their vagueness: clear or bright, blessed, worthy, praised, and candid. This modesty is also extended to the imagery of the poem. Bitterness has turned to sweetness, for night has made her life content, "restoring him who bound me to my arms" (CIV). The most audacious line of this text, it too is so innocent that one of Stampa's defenders in the critical polemics of the early twentieth century read it to mean that they did no more than pass the evening together in conversation and fond embrace after their long separation. Such an interpretation is naive and basically ignores the sensual undercurrent present throughout the "Rime d'Amore," but it does point to the lack of eroticism in the Stampian choice of vocabulary. There is only one sexual suggestion that is overt: in the first tercet, the poet regrets that, not as fortunate as Alcmena, she could not delay the coming of the dawn. Although nothing is stated, much is suggested by this mythological allusion. Phoebus has delayed daybreak so Alcmena and Jove might delight in their ecstasy awhile longer. But no mention is made in Stampa's poem of either the celestial lover or the purpose of such a boon.

Termed a "fallen woman's hymn" by Benedetto Croce, poem CLVIII is a call to the lover to spend his life with her in love, with no other cares. The *carpe diem* theme is developed as an invitation to relish the beauties of nature in felicitous harmony. It is certainly no more indecent or obscene—Croce notwithstanding—than the poetry of later English writers, like Spenser, Marlowe, Herrick, and Marvel. The theme itself is of classical origins, notably Horatian. It is a call to enjoy the joys of love and beauty before they vanish in time and death. Although contrary to the Petrarchan celebration of chastity and spiritual love, this pagan motif is in keeping with Renaissance mores and literary tradition:

> Deh lasciate, signor, le maggior cure
> d'ir procacciando in questa età fiorita
> con fatiche e perigilio de la vita
> alti pregi, alti onori, alte venture;

e in questi colli, in queste alme e sicure
valli e campagne, dove Amore n'invita,
viviamo insieme vita alma e gradita,
fin che 'l sol de' nostr'occhi alfin s'oscure.
Perché tante fatiche e tanti stenti
fan la vita più dura, e tanti onori
restan per morte poi subito spenti.
Qui coglieremo a tempo e rose e fiori,
ed erbe e frutti, e con dolci concenti
canterem con gli uccelli i nostri amori. (CLVIII)

(Ah! my lord, leave those heavy cares whereby you seek great
rewards, great honors, and great fortune, with toil and danger to
your life, while you are young! Amid these hills, these fertile,
sheltered valleys and fields, where Love invites, let's spend a sublime
and happy life together 'til the light of our eyes grows dim. So
much effort and so much toil make life harder, and so many honors
will soon be snuffed out by death. In time we'll gather roses and
flowers and leaves and fruit here, and with sweet harmony we'll
sing our loves along with the birds.)

Traces of desire blossom here and there in Stampa's other poetry, but
sensuality does not give way to actual lust. A child of this earthly
flame, the green-eyed monster of jealousy reappears often in the
poetry. An uncommon theme in the spiritualizing lyric poets of the
Middle Ages, jealousy is a real presence in the more materialistic
Renaissance. It appears in a variety of situations typical of the *Rime;*
the fears of a new love on the horizon, aggravated by lengthy
separations and the possibility of abandonment, are its major cause.
Jealousy is correlative to fear and a manifestation of pain. It is also
indicative of the force of her love. To protect herself and her peace of
mind, Gaspara pleads, invokes, demands, begs, and accuses the
supposedly wandering beloved: "Is this the joy I hoped from you? Is
this what you've said to me? Is this the faith you've promised me?"
(LXXVII). The motif signals a duality in the presentation of the lover
as well; it is representative of his inherent negativity.

Throughout the *Rime,* the figure of the beloved, Collaltino, is
ambiguous, undergoing a contemporaneous process of idealization and

denigration. Presented initially as a perfect being, an idealized hero, and the fount of all virtues, the beloved is also immediately defective. The first sonnet of praise (IV) makes this dilemma clear. After singing his many qualities, associated with the planetary influences, Stampa goes on to note the "coldness" given him by the moon. The final tercet announces the dichotomy between the two protagonists of this love story, a dichotomy which will dominate the thematic content of the entire work: "Each of these many and rare graces inflamed me with my noble flame, and that single one (the moon's) was left to turn him to ice." The larger antithesis between Gaspara (flame) and the count (ice) upon which the movement of the *Rime* is founded is reflected in the inner contradiction in the beloved himself. His facade of "loyal and benign" lord which extends to all his deeds, thoughts, person, and essence, is in gross contradiction with her own negative image of him: "I carry you engraved, as I've known you in deed, a bit fickle and a bit proud" (LVII). This opposition of "countenance" and "deed" is responsible for much of the dramatic tension underlying the love poetry. The conflict is staged between an idealized source of love (the Platonic and Petrarchan influences) and the reality of his human fallibility. Collaltino is both idol and sadist, Platonic sun and demonic assassin. His flaws give rise to pain, torment, suffering, doubt, jealousy, and frustration. His perfections elicit love and worship.

Stampa's pain is not like Petrarca's, born of the realization of the unattainability of love. It is engendered of the exasperation of love attained and found wanting, yet always desirable as the greatest possible realization. The intensity of this pain, stemming from the contradictory nature of both the beloved and love, suffuses the poetry. It is the voice of anguish, unrequited devotion, quest, humility, degradation, and self-destruction. To borrow a metaphor, Stampa's poetry is "dressed in mourning."[4] Ominous shadows collect around the *persona* even in the beloved's presence. Jealousy embitters the fleeting moments of joy and serenity. Like Petrarca, before her, the poet is deeply aware of the temporality of all things. Nothing is secure in Stampa's world. Even during her moments of requited love, she muses on their "uncertain and fleeting" delights. Poems, such as CVII, begin with images of birth, renewal, and life, like spring bringing love after a winter of discontent, only to conclude in intimations of loss, as day gives way to evening, spring to winter. In Stampa's verse, the negative is generally inherent in the positive. The light of day suggests the darkness of night; presence implies absence; love, abandon. Her sorrowful refrains are far more numerous than her paeans, for joy fulfills by its very nature while pain cries out for expression, compassion, and understanding.

In a love composed more of separation than intimacy, desperation inevitably becomes its key note. Hope gives way to despair and hopelessness brings on thoughts of death, frustration, solitude, and impotence. Stampa's poetry is replete with images of unending dreariness, unlighted gloom, and mourning, in a fitting resolution of the light metaphor, for darkness must follow once one's "sun" is gone. Death is a frequent visitor in Gaspara's pages. It is the obvious solution to her unresolved antithetical condition, being an apt substitute for love. Death is the poet's exit from this unbearable state into a realm of peace where all contradictions have been resolved. As poets from time immemorial have known, love and death are closely interwoven in the fabric of life and art. Stampa interprets this interplay poetically to symbolize the power of the beloved; if he rejects her and takes away his love, death is the obvious result. Thus, he wields the power of life and death because life without love is no more than a living death. Love also possesses another quality akin to death's; both create solitude and isolation. Through her ability to love, she is "unique" among all others, but this singularity has its price: no one can share her joys or her pains. The same holds true for death; it must be met alone. This friendless state which accompanies both death and love is poignantly rendered in poem LXI: "Who will come to my aid in my last hour, when death will come to take me from this life? . . . Mother and sister, no, for fear invites them both to grieve with me, and as I well know, their aid does not avail this last great woe." Finding herself alone, with no visible remedy, and facing death or the loss of love, the poet reverts to images of dissolution and doom.

The inherent impotence of the lover leads fatalistically to the sense of impending disintegration. The poet captures this process by adopting the mythological symbol of Echo—repeated a number of times in the *Rime,* alongside that of the Chimera—to incarnate her idea. The dissolution of the self through the pain of loving is aptly depicted in the disappearance of the physical body which is transformed into an immaterial voice. The tone of fatalism is strengthened by the employment of astrological imagery. Whereas planetary influences had been used to signify the positive qualities of the count's character, the stars as well as the elements conspire to prepare her misfortune: "Air, sea, earth, heavens, sun, stars, and moon, each with its pride and might, have moved to do me injury and ruin . . . since my cradle days" (LX). Thus doomed, she cannot react, but only accept. Love is the bearer of death, willingly embraced, "I see myself dying and I consent to it" (LXIX). Pain is both justified and welcomed as a necessary appendix to the love of so superior a being as she has chosen or, rather, as has chosen her. "Ruling suits him; serving, me, so humble and base a woman; it even seems a great boon to me that he not disdain my suffering for him" (CXLVIII).

The acceptance of the negativity innate in loving is so complete that pleasure and pain form one sensation. Stampa's masochism is derived from her complacency; suffering pleases her as long as such pain is the product of love, "for Love's miseries are blessed" (XXIV). The motif is Petrarchan in origin, but Stampa intensifies it and expands it until it is one of the thematic pillars upon which the "Rime d'Amore" rest. It is an addition to the already present antitheses forming the internal structure of the love poetry: positive versus negative love, Gaspara versus Collaltino, the godlike beloved versus the human and flawed man, joy versus suffering, and so forth. Once again, love appears as the reigning power in the text; it is proposed as the greatest possible good, even when it is bad. The imperious nature of love is often captured through the sound and phrasing of the Stampian line, as shown in the hammering tempo of the following anaphoric construction based on the imperative—grammatically and intentionally—mood:

> Straziami, Amor, se sai, dammi tormento,
> tommi pur lui, che vorrei sempre presso,
> tommi pur, crudo e disleal, con esso
> ogni mia pace ed ogni mio contento,
>   fammi pur mesta e lieta in un momento,
> dammi più morti con un colpo stesso,
> fammi essempio infelice del mio sesso,
> che per ciò di seguirti non mi pento. (CLIV)

(Tear me apart, Love, if you can; give me torments; take him away,
whom I would always wish nearby; take with him, cruel and unfair
Love, my every peace and my every joy; make me melancholy and
gay at once; give me many deaths in a single blow; make me the
unhappy specimen of my sex; for all that, I don't regret having
followed you.)

The energy of this sonnet lies in its excess and stress. The emphatic
flow of emotions bursts from the page in the rapid pace of the musical
crescendo, overpowering the controlled limits established in Petrarchan
imitation, where decorum and restraint were essential attributes. With
this poem and others like it, Stampa has entered the unruly and
extravagant world of the hyperbole, where exaggeration and amplifi-
cation hold sway. The poet's use of exaggeration is an outgrowth of
her tendency to antithetical constructions and images. "Stampa's
hyperbole is developed through the conflict of feelings; it flows
exclusively into their representation along contoured and taut lines."[5]
Exasperation, frustration, passion, fixation on the beloved or on love,
anger, and reproach are voiced through the rhetorical device of the
hyperbole, which exists on extremes. Excess breeds excess, ignoring
the conventions of composure and artistic serenity so treasured by
Petrarca and Bembo. Contradictory feelings, the tensions and extremes
of emotion, and the praise of the beloved are all dramatized through
language. Gaspara Stampa's use of the hyperbole is never purely
rhetorical, divorced from thought or content as often happens in the
baroque poets; it retains its ties with the subject matter at hand and
serves as a linguistic tool in the depiction of images, states of mind and
being, emotions, personalities, and situations.

To describe her unhappiness, Gaspara notes that her tears and sighs
could overcome the most tempest-tossed seas, while his heart, "a fierce
tiger's or a serpent's heart," feeds on her suffering (LIX). Hyperbole
serves to emphasize the extremes of Collaltino's contradictory character. He is "the world's sole monster (prodigy)" (LXIII) or, conversely,
"a bear or tiger's heart." To depict her sufferings, Stampa declares
that she is worse off than an "accused man condemned to death, to
exile, to chains, for another's sin." Exaggeration also illustrates her
capacity to love. Compared to her own flame, those that burned Troy

or those that Etna vomited are relatively "peace and joy" (LXXV). Her passionate fire puts the sufferings of hell to scorn, "altogether they are little or naught" (CCXXXI). Her tears can cause the sea to rise (CXLIX) while his cruelty towards her can turn her into a Chimera, a chaotic abyss, or an unnaturally stormy sea (CLXXIV). The majority of poems in praise of the beloved also fall into the category of overstatement, as is typical of the entire code of courtly love, whose central aim is to exalt the lady (or gentleman) one has chosen to love. Some of Stampa's compositions border on idolatry, if not sacrilege. Neo-Platonism also prepared the terrain for such hyperbole, with its spiritual apotheosis of the beloved and emphasis on the existence of perfect ideas or entities (the good, the true, the beautiful). In keeping with her election of a corporeal rather than spiritual ideal, the poet uses religious imagery to depict human states, thus forming a hyperbolic context. Her soul would go to heaven, save that "its true and proper paradise, the one in which it chose to rejoice, is my sweet lord and his handsome face" (XXIX). Nor does she envy the angels who delight in the sight of God, for "as you are wont to enjoy great solace and life from His countenance in heaven, so do I here below, from his infinite beauty" (XVII). Thus, she has created an earthly paradise for herself, drawn from a hyperbolic interpretation of Platonic concepts. God and Collaltino fuse, for his beauty, like the Almighty's, is infinite and beauty is, after all, synonymous with good. Once again, Stampa has adroitly used language (the rhetorical device of the hyperbole) to convey and complement meaning. Nor would the poet's exaggerated praises of the beloved be complete without equally overstated denunciations of his cruelty and indifference. Often, these are mingled with a fair dose of irony, as in poem XCIV wherein he, the mighty warrior attacks the defenseless, makes the surrenderer cower, and combats the dead, while she would willingly be a slave herded in front of his victory chariot, or in XCVII: "Oh wondrous valor of a gentle knight to have carried the heart of an imprudent maiden all the way to France!" An exceptional example of Stampa's application of poetic devices is sonnet CXLII, which integrates hyperbole, irony, direct address, rhetorical questions, prosaic tone, mythological imagery, Neo-Platonic symbolism, and an everyday situation:

Rimandatemi il cor, empio tiranno,
ch'a sì gran torto avete ed istraziate,
e di lui e di me quel proprio fate,
che le tigri e i leon di cerva fanno.
  Son passati otto giorni, a me un anno,
ch'io non ho vostre lettre od imbasciate,
contra le fé che voi m'avete date,
o fonte di valor, conte, e d'inganno.
  Credete ch'io sia Ercol o Sansone
a poter sostener tanto dolore,
giovane e donna e fuor d'ogni ragione,
    massime essendo qui senza 'l mio core
e senza voi a mia difensione,
onde mi suol venir forza e vigore? (CXLII)

(Send back my heart, cruel tyrant, which you wrongfully hold and
tear apart, doing to it and me what tigers and lions do to stags.
Eight days have passed, a year to me, and I've had no letters or
news of you, contrary to the promises you made me, oh font of
gallantry and deceit, oh count! Do you take me for Hercules or
Samson, to bear such pain, I, young, a woman, and unsettled in my
mind, especially since I am here without my heart and without you
to come to my defense, you, from whom I am wont to receive my
strength and vigor?)

Love's Phoenix

The love poems written for Bartolomeo Zen repeat and renew many
of Stampa's stylistic procedures and basic themes and imagery. The
existence of this second passion emphasized the prominence of love as
the central focus of the *Rime,* rather than the figure of the beloved.
The unifying force behind this *canzoniere* is the poetic fixation on love
and loving, rather than the influence of one specific emotional
attachment. The man only serves to embody the source of love and the
direction it takes. This amatory inspiration is the conceptual thread
connecting all the compositions forming the "Rime d'Amore," even
when the love object changes. Although not unheard of, the singing of
two beloveds in the space of one collection was hardly in keeping with
the Petrarchan model. The vague possibility of a new flame to replace

Collaltino was heralded earlier in the *Rime* in a sonnet of jealousy. To eliminate such a negative condition, Gaspara poetically suggested two options. The first, and typically Stampian, manner was sublimation through art: "let there be an outlet for my sighs, let poetry be written, so that such evil grief be given vent" (CXXVII). The other solution is less lofty but far more practical, for she will find another lover: "I will take another love, and leave this one for which I blaze." This sensible exchange is eloquently, if commonly, expressed in Gaspara's paraphrase of an old proverb which states that *chiodo schiacca chiodo* ("one nail [pain] drives out another") or, in her own words, *foco scaccia foco* ("one fire drives out another"), as she declares in poem CCXIV when the substitution has already been completed.

What had only been a vague possibility and a psychological ploy in the earlier sonnet is realized in the final poems of the "Rime d'Amore" (CCVII–CCXXI). The first of these compositions is transitional, being addressed to Amor rather than the new beloved. It presents an inner conflict between the desire for freedom and the appeal of love. It is a brief emotional truce, quickly broken in one of the most popular of Stampa's poems. While the previous sonnet pleads with Amor for peace, a more tempered flame, and a piteous lover, CCVIII is a paean to loving, burning, and suffering:

> Amor m'ha fatto tal ch'io vivo in foco,
> qual nova salamandra al mondo, e quale
> l'altro di lei non men stranio animale,
> che vive e spira nel medesmo loco.
>   Le mie delizie son tutte e 'l mio gioco
> viver ardendo e non sentire il male,
> e non curar ch'ei che m'induce a tale
> abbia di me pietà molto né poco.

(Love has made me such that I live in fire, like a second salamander in this world and like that other equally strange beast that lives and dies in the same place [the pheonix]. All my delights and my game are to live in flames and never feel the pain and never care if he who leads me to this, pities me little or much.)

The sonnet is a declaration of her existential reality; she is a creature of love, destined to passion and pain.[6] Here and elsewhere in the poems to Zen, many typically Stampian themes reappear: the ineluctable power of love, the subordination of self to the beloved, the *voluptas dolendi,* the antithesis of joy and pain, the *topos* of the victim or prey of love, and the masochistic pleasure of submission. But these two loves are not identical or interchangeable. Whereas dissolution and death had underscored the imagery associated with the first passion, rebirth punctuates the second. The two opposing symbols of these loves are the nymph Echo and the phoenix or the salamander. These last two legendary beasts are both associated with fire (love); the latter lives in flames unharmed and invulnerable, the former is a miraculous bird fabled to live for five hundred years, consume itself in its own fire, only to rise fresh and renewed from its ashes. In Stampa's poetry, this emblem of immortality is elevated to the symbol of her own loving which, once dead, is fated to reappear.

But love's renewal is not without struggle and psychological conflict. The protagonist ponders and weighs the options of loving or not loving, always returning to the image of herself as predestined prey or foreordained victim, thus repeating the vision of herself as a weak pawn in the hands of a mighty king, a lord who has power over her life. It is, of course, a process of poetic self-justification as the *persona* excuses or rationalizes her choices before the fact. Drawing from the Petrarchan concept of love as war and her own previous employment of military images to describe Collaltino and their contrasted love, Stampa creates a bellicose allegory. Amor is a belligerent warrior in the battlefield of love, penetrating any armor (resistance). In this campaign waged against her the protagonist concludes that "retreat is safe, resistance glorious," while the "bait" offered can both "benefit and damage at once." This last antithesis is resolved in favor of doing battle, "you can neither win nor lose if you do not joust" (CCXII). This long allegory of love's war is representative of the type of rhetorical techniques the poet employed in these sonnets. Much of the hyperbolic language associated with the love for Collaltino reappears. She will once again fall into "a sea of tears" (CCXIII); the count makes an appearance as "that alpine and hardened heart, colder than the coldest slopes of snow," while her old wound resembles a volcano, "it awakens now and then and flares up, and now and then it hurls blood and humors" (CCXIV). But it is the unusual religious tone and the array of Christian images which sets these compositions apart, for this second love—more than the first—is strangely interpreted through spiritual terms. The contamination of religion and carnal love is natural to all Stampa's poetry because of its Petrarchan and Neo-Platonic origins. But whereas most of Stampa's religious symbolism had merely served as a tool in the apotheosis of Collaltino, in accord with the Platonic doctrines popular in her age, it pursues a different direction in the poetry directed to Zen. Religion is used in the attempt to convince the beloved to reciprocate her love, not to praise his virtues or elevate him. She borrows from the Scriptures to emphasize her point, using the figure of Jesus as an accomplice in her seduction of a hesitant courter. Love, Gaspara's supreme good, exploits all available means to persuade and cajole, even the Gospels: " 'Love who hates you,' our Lord cries from afar, 'not only who loves you,' He, who opened the way for our ascent to heaven from his cross" (CCXVII). Religiosity has been reinterpreted to serve a purely secular and doubtlessly erotic end. Christ himself becomes the instrument of Amor—the greater god in these poems—for only Amor can provide that paradise on earth attainable through the mutual sharing of love. This distorted evangelical theme is repeated and extended in another sonnet. The poet asks her beloved where he plans to direct his hopes and desires, in order to be worthy of her love:

> Forse a Dio? Già da Dio non si diparte
> chi d'Amor segue la felice insegna:
> Ei di sua bocca propria pur c'insegna
> ad amar lui e 'l prossimo in disparte.
>   Or, se devete amar, non è via meglio
> amar me, che v'adoro e che ho fatto
> del vostro vago viso tempio e speglio?
>   Dunque amate, e servate, amando, il patto
> c'ha fatto Cristo; ed amando io vi sveglio
> che amiate cor, che ad amar voi sia atto. (CCXVIII)

(Perhaps to God? But you cannot depart from God by following
Love's happy banner: with his own words, He teaches us to love
him and our neighbor too. Now, if you must love, what better way
is there than by loving me, for I adore you and I've made a temple
and mirror of your lovely face? Love then; and, by loving, keep
Christ's pact; and loving I rouse you to love a heart capable of
loving you.)

Sacred and profane mix, as Christ and Amor blend and sensuality
unites with religious mystery. Unlike Collaltino, Zen is not an idol or
a god, but a temple where she can celebrate the liturgy of love. So
intertwined are faith and passion in these poems, that her feelings are
described in terms of *caritas* rather than *eros:* "It is fit that we both be
equally inflamed with the zeal of ardent charity in our sweet and
loving burden" (CCXIX). This blending of Christian and pagan
notions serves to create a new ideal, distinct from the cold indifference
and cruelty of the first love. This new passion seeks the tranquil and
stable affection which has the earmarks of a sanctified union, based on
"charity, peace, faith, and humility," and recognized by all: " 'O
happy and sublime couple, the stars are your gracious friends, so
sweetly are you united in one will!' " (CCXX). But the conclusion of
this second rapport is very like the first's; she has gone "from one fire
to another, from one to another pain" (CCXXI). The attempt to
spiritualize is ambiguous and therefore unsuccessful. Amor is the sole
victor in this poetic world where Christ plays Cupid, men become gods,
and love's hell is the lover's chosen paradise.

Closing Remarks

Gaspara Stampa was not a professional writer or a prolific poet.
Only one book, a collection of poems legitimately titled *Rime,* recalls
her avocation and her very existence. And this one book can only
suggest the author's finest artistic maturity and future potentials.
Published as a posthumous tribute by a few loyal admirers and a
loving sister, the *Rime*—although copied from the autograph—had
obviously not yet achieved the final form desired by the poet who was
polishing and assembling it at the time of her death. Even in its
imperfect state, Stampa's *Rime* is a unique *canzoniere,* which gives

modern readers a full and exciting picture of the poet's personality, her aspirations and inspirations, the historical—literary and social— factors that shaped her, her ideals, and her artistic defects and accomplishments. It is the key to the understanding of a woman, a writer, and a time.

Writers—novelists, poets, essayists, historians, memorialists, and playwrights alike—all offer not only their works but also their existence to criticism, analysis, and dissection. The act of producing words on a page for the eyes, ears, and minds of others is a public denudation at various stages of undress. Some writers offer themselves freely to such personal scrutiny, transforming their lives and their very beings into literature. In the process, the tale of self becomes the tale of everyman, a universal rather than a spiritual experience. Other writers create fictions of themselves. Still others draw attention to their biographies by nature of their identities, because of who and what they are. Among these number kings, saints, great sinners, and . . . women. The woman writer is both victim and victimizer of her sex. Stereotyped as a woman far more readily and quickly than as a writer, she and her writing are categorized as sensitive, intuitive, emotional, and subjective. A woman writer is just that, first a woman and second a writer. Her works are often approached not as artistic products of a specific time, class, mentality, and place, but as the reflections of a woman's biographical experience, making them different and detached from literature in general.

Gaspara Stampa the writer has often been ignored in favor of the woman. The mysterious figure intrigued many through the centuries. Some, like Carrer, gloried in the lack of data, which permitted the creation of sentimental fiction. Others, like Salza, sought to demolish the myth through scholarship. A few, like Croce, pooh-poohed the biographical polemics—was she or was she not a courtesan—but patronizingly defined her poetry "feminine." Gaspara Stampa was indeed a woman. But more importantly, she was a writer who wrote as a woman of the sixteenth-century Venetian Renaissance. As such, she belonged to a privileged group of ladies, matrons, *virtuose,* aristocrats, and courtesans who actively participated in the cultural life of her city. For the first time in the history of Italian literature, women contributed significantly to the composition and diffusion of poetry, prose, and general culture. Educated if not emancipated, they sought prestige and a certain celebrity through art. Gaspara Stampa was one of them and, like them, she mirrored the taste, cultivation, refinement, and ideals of her era.

Art means different things to different times, for it is both a personal expression unrelated to any period and a historical phenomenon. Stampa's art is no exception. While she could be innovative, she was not an innovator. Her poems, like those of her contemporaries, were born under the sign of Petrarchismo and imitation, which would continue to influence Italian lyric poetry well into the nineteenth century. Consecrated in Bembo's theoretical works, the Petrarchan code became the poetic idiom of the day, the language in which verse was written and love was discussed. Tradition was sacred, and Stampa respected it by imitating it. The *Canzoniere* offered the techniques, the diction, the rhetorical devices, and the motifs; the poets of the Cinquecento reworded them hoping to arrive at the best possible literary effects and the most polished formal apparatus achievable. They were fundamentally classicists attracted to decorum, composure, and contemplation. Many of Stampa's themes and much of her language is directly borrowed from the great master. Her *Rime* follow the standard format of a *canzoniere*. The conventional motifs are the same: the beauty and cruelty of the lover, resulting in torments and the fear of death. Nor was Stampa an intuitive writer, a primitive. Any analysis of her poetry shows an artist familiar with the devices of her craft, cognizant of the apparatus of rhetoric and the complexities of prosody and quite capable of utilizing them.

The Renaissance was captivated by beauty. It was desired in art, resulting in a highly developed aesthetic sensibility, and it was sought in life. This led to the period's attraction to Platonism, where beauty was joined to other abstract ideals, such as love and truth. Inevitably, Platonic concepts and Petrarchan motifs intermingled and fused in the literature of the Cinquecento. The idea of beauty or love came to be worshiped as a more significant object of reverence than the physical woman (or man) in whom it was embodied. Stampa clearly understood these notions. The poet did not possess vast knowledge nor were her studies extensive or profound, but she was aware of the Neo-Platonic issues of her day, if only through the popular treatises on love and salon discussions. She understood and translated thought into poetic motifs and images: the apotheosis of the count, the omnipotence of Amor, the unbreakable union of physical charms and love, and the metamorphosis of the corporeal man into abstract image.

Seen in this light, the *Rime* is a significant work for it contains the ideals, literary expectations, conventions, motifs, and language of the lyric poetry of a century. It is a document of import for any modern reader who wishes to familiarize himself with the literature of the Italian Renaissance, the nature of Petrarchismo, the interaction of Neo-Platonism and poetry, or the role of women writers in the sixteenth century. But the *Rime* is also a work of art, which can present itself on its own merits, in or out of a purely historical context. Produced in an era dominated by Petrarchan imitation and rhetoric, it stands out for its lack of affectation, its often unpolished voice of sincerity, and its emotional excesses. It is perhaps the only *canzoniere* of the many written in the sixteenth century where the personal and biographical elements sound a vital note, in contrast to the monotonous repetition of the ordinary imitations. In the midst of her own literariness, Gaspara Stampa produces the sense of a throbbing vitality, a human presence, which expresses itself through a variety of poetic techniques and tones, ranging from pure musical cadences to hyperbolic exclamations, from prosaic speech patterns to the hammering staccato beat of the repeated anaphoras.

Just as the rhythms and sounds of Stampa's poetry are rich and varied, so too does she offer a wealth of psychological nuances to explore. Poetry is concerned with feelings, reactions, and attitudes, as well as with meter and rhyme. The *Rime* are a treasure trove where one can discover the entire emotional drama of love being enacted: rapture, jealousy, hope, anxiety, desire, satiation, worry, rejection, sublimation, and more. And the whole is held together by a unifying network of images around a central theme. This tale of love is not a mere love story in verse. It is the depiction of a universal motif of literature and of a moving force in human life: Love. For this reason it continues to attract an audience. It elicits not only the rational and intellectual reactions of the literary scholar, but also the emotional response of the ordinary reader. It is poetry for the heart and the mind, just as Gaspara Stampa is a poet for all times.

Notes and References

Chapter One

1. Cf. Ruth Kelso, *Doctrine for the Lady of the Renaissance* (Urbana: University of Illinois Press, 1956), p. 71. Although not exclusively devoted to the Italian environment, Kelso's book offers an excellent view of the position of women in fifteenth-and sixteenth-century culture, including an analysis of their training, studies, readings, and status. Other fine texts dealing with the position and education of women in the Renaissance in Italy are Sidney Alexander, "Women of the Renaissance," in *Lions and Foxes: Men and Ideas of the Italian Renaissance* (New York: Macmillan, 1974), and André Rochon, "L'Italienne: Eve jugée par Adam," in *Histoire mondiale de la femme: L'Occident, des Celtes a la Renaissance* (Paris: Nouvelle Librairie de France, 1966), II, 213–304. For a view of polite society, its interests and readings, see Thomas Frederick Crane, *Italian Social Customs of the Sixteenth Century* (New Haven: Yale University Press, 1920). Chattier works which offer some information and sketches of famous women and their life-style are Maud Jerrold, *Italy in the Renaissance* (Boston: John W. Luce, 1928); Emily Putnam, *The Lady* (Chicago-London: University of Chicago Press, 1938); Rachel Annand Taylor, "Women of the Renaissance," in *Invitation to Renaissance Italy* (New York: Harper, 1930); and Christopher Hare, *The Most Illustrious Ladies of the Italian Renaissance* (New York: Scribners, 1904).

2. Kelso, p. 30.

3. See Gioachino Brognoligo, "Gaspara Stampa," *Giornale storico della letteratura italiana* 76 (1920):134–43, and Maria Bellonci's "Introduzione" to Gaspara Stampa, *Rime*, 2nd ed. (Milano, 1976). The possibility for this musical profession is suggested both by the comments of Stampa's contemporaries on her musical abilities, by some of Stampa's own poetry dedicated to the subject of singing, and by a letter written by Lucrezia Gonzaga in 1552 to Ortensio Lando, in which she discusses a sonnet by the poet: "I read the sonnet composed by the *virtuosa* Madonna Gaspara Stampa in your honor more than a thousand times. . . . " The pertinent passages from this letter are quoted in the above-cited edition of the *Rime*, p. 56.

4. See Brian Pullan, *Rich and Poor in Renaissance Venice* (Cambridge, Mass.: Harvard University Press, 1971), p. 415.

5. For additional information of the role of music and the position of musicians in sixteenth-century Italy, see Jacob Burckhardt, *The Civilization of the Renaissance in Italy* (New York: Harper, 1958), II, 385–88, and Will Durant, *The Renaissance: A History of Civilization in Italy from 1304–1576 A.D.* (New York: Simon and Schuster, 1953), pp. 598–601.

6. All documents concerning Gaspara Stampa, including letters, poetry, and biographical sketches, are cited by Abdelkader Salza in his serious and key studies on the poet. Any future references to these Renaissance sources will be from these studies: "Madonna Gasparina Stampa secondo nuove indagini," *Giornale storico della letteratura italiana* 62 (1913):1–101, and "Madonna Gasparina Stampa e la società veneziana del suo tempo," *Giornale storico della letteratura italiana* 70 (1917): 1–60, 281–99. The poetry dedicated to Stampa by her contemporaries is presented in one of the appendices, "Rime di diversi," to Salza's edition of Gaspara Stampa and Veronica Franco, *Rime* (Bari, 1913), pp. 187–96. Some of this material is also presented in the "Documenti" section of the 1976 Rizzoli edition of the *Rime,* pp. 55–62.

7. James Cushman Davis, *The Decline of the Venetian Nobility as a Ruling Class,* Johns Hopkins University Studies in Historical and Political Science, Series LXXX, No. 2 (Baltimore: Johns Hopkins Press, 1962), p. 15. For more information on the Venetian nobility, the city's government, the class structure, and general atmosphere, consult D. S. Chambers, *The Imperial Age of Venice: 1380–1580* (London: Thames and Hudson, 1970); Oliver Logan, *Culture and Society in Venice 1470–1790* (London: Batsford Ltd., 1972); William H. McNeill, *Venice the Hinge of Europe 1081–1797* (Chicago: University of Chicago Press, 1974); J. H. Plumb, "Venice, the Golden Years," in *The Italian Renaissance* (New York: Harper and Row, 1961), pp. 95–109; Brian Pullan, *Rich and Poor;* and Angelo Ventura, *Nobiltà e popolo nella società veneta del '400 e '500* (Bari: Laterza, 1964).

8. Matteo Bandello, *Tutte le opere,* ed. Francesco Flora, 3rd ed. (Milano: Mondadori, 1952), II, 417. Bandello's short stories are a treasure-trove for anyone interested in the sixteenth century, for they depict the life and tone of the courts and salons in the introductions to each tale, as well as giving descriptions of mores, entertainments, conversations, real people, and actual events. The stories themselves are excellent indicators of the taste, mentality, and ideals of the late Renaissance. A good number of them are set in and around Venice as well. Other texts which describe the life of sixteenth-century Italy are Paul Burke, *Culture and Society in Renaissance Italy 1420–1540* (New York: Scribner's, 1972); John Gage, *Life in Italy at the Time of the Medici* (London: Putnam, 1968); Will Durant, *The Renaissance;* and

Paul Renucci, "La cultura," in *Storia d'Italia: dalla caduta dell'Impero Romano al secolo XVIII,* ed. Ruggiero Romano and Corrado Vivanti (Torino: Einaudi, 1974), II, No. 2, 1085–1463. A seminal work, Burckhardt's *Civilization of the Renaissance,* although first published in the mid-1800s, is still required reading for anyone interested in that period of Italian culture.

9. Baldassare Stampa's friends and correspondents include Anton Francesco Doni, the best-known Bohemian writer of the century; Lodovico Domenichi, noted *poligrafo* and poet; and Francesca Baffo, one of Venice's most famous female intellectuals and liberated women.

10. Francesco Sansovino's *Ragionamento* is to be found in *Trattati d'amore del Cinquecento,* ed. Giuseppe Zonta (Bari: Laterza, 1912), pp. 151–84. The text has been reprinted by Laterza in 1975, edited by Mario Pozzi.

11. A great number of such academies sprang up in the fifteenth and sixteenth centuries. The name was first applied to the Platonic Academy of Florence, but their popularity quickly spread to Rome and Venice. The earlier groups were devoted to classical studies, like Aldus Manutius's Neacademia, involved in the discovery of the ancients. Later on, these academies became more and more interested in the discussion of poetry and Italian literature. The names of such clubs tend to be bizarre: the Gelati ("Frozen Ones"), the Accesi ("Inflamed"), the Ricoverati ("Recovered Ones"), and so forth. Very little is actually known of the Pellegrini ("Pilgrims"), save their interest in literary matters. No documentation survives and some critics have even doubted the academy's existence.

12. Logan, p. 94.

13. Cf. Chambers, pp. 137–38.

14. Among the solutions for the *questione della lingua,* or choice of a literary tongue, one of the favored was Baldassare Castiglione's suggestion that the *lingua cortegiana,* the vernacular employed in the courts, be chosen. But the linguistic and literary situation in Venice was unique, in part because—given the lack of a true aristocracy—no courts existed. The Venetians used their dialect not only for oral communications, but in state and private documents as well. In fact, a rich literature of Petrarchan sonnets in Venetian dialect of the Cinquecento exists. Fifteenth-century academies had generally employed Latin in conversation, but the use of the ancient tongue was not extensive among the general population in a city dedicated to the pursuit of commerce, not culture. The invention of the printing press, however, and the eventual development of Venice as the printing capital of Europe required the establishment of a written language suited to the needs

of this new intellectual environment. It is not surprising that the city would become one of the major centers of this linguistic debate.

15. Gaspara Stampa and Veronica Franco, *Rime,* ed. Abdelkader Salza (Bari, 1913), p. 152, poem CCLXIII. This Salza edition, being the most available and accurate modern source, will be used for quoting from Stampa's poetry. To avoid lengthy notes or references, all selections from the *Rime* will be cited in the body of the text with their numbers, in roman numerals. The two latest editions of Stampa's poetry, published by Rizzoli in 1954 and 1976, both follow the Salza model.

16. The Collalto family was feudal nobility in both blood and deed. Collaltino himself was banished from the Venetian Republic for having formed an illegal private army to be used against his own relatives. For this act, he was forced into exile at the Gonzaga court in Mantua, where he died. His sons apparently followed in his footsteps. In 1585, Pirro and Furio Camillo attacked the Castle of Collalto, being defended by the widow of a relative, also with a small army of their own. This caused great public scandal and resulted in a sensational trial initiated by the State against the Collalto brothers (see Angelo Ventura, p. 339).

17. Plumb, p. 129.

18. Cf. Burckhardt, p. 360. The equality the great historian sees in the Italian Renaissance among men of all classes may well have existed on an intellectual plane, but apparently did not filter down into the economic or political sector. Blood and money still prevailed, although more room at the top was made for genius and culture.

19. A few existing correspondence sonnets, written by Stampa's acquaintances, testify to the fact that the two were recognized socially as a couple. Among them, a poem dedicated to Collaltino, in which Girolamo Molin mentions a woman "who sings and sighs so sweetly, that winter will be forever banished from you. She, and you with her, will be first among all illustrious women who ever wrote of their flames in prose or rhyme with a noble vein."

20. Elisa Innocenzi Greggio, "In difesa di Gaspara Stampa," *L'Ateneo Veneto* 38, I (1915): 28. Next to Salza's scholarly works, this article is the finest piece of historical research done on Stampa.

21. The publication of this death certificate added fuel to the critical debate between Salza and Stampa's defenders in the early decades of this century. Since Salza held to his opinion that Gaspara had been a courtesan, he sought to prove that probable cause of death was a gynecological illness, possibly puerperal fever, basing himself on sixteenth- and seventeenth-century medical definitions or mentions of *mal de mare* ("matrix pains"). See

Abdelkader Salza, "Madonna Gasparina Stampa e la società veneziana del suo tempo," *Giornale storico della letteratura italiana* 62(1913):281–88. Another critic, G. A. Cesareo, rebutted in *Gaspara Stampa donna e poetessa* (Napoli, 1920), p. 51 (footnote 2), by presenting contemporary as well as ancient medical evidence for a disease including fever, abdominal and matrix pains. His sound—medically if not critically—conclusion was that poor Gaspara died of appendicitis, complicated by peritonitis, "a lethal but very honest infirmity."

22. Quoted in the "Nota" to Gaspara Stampa and Veronica Franco, pp. 368–69.

Chapter Two

1. See Durant, p. 315, and Renucci, pp. 1270–71, for more information on printing and book publication in Venice.

2. Quoted in the "Documenti" section of 1976 edition of Stampa's *Rime*. Before the appearance of the second edition of Stampa's poetry, the Renaissance writer had been mentioned in a few literary encyclopedias. Alessandro Zilioli included an entry on the poet in his *Vite*, written some fifty years after her death, while Apostolo Zeno discussed her briefly in an appendix to Fontanini's *Eloquenza Italiana* that appeared in the first part of the eighteenth century. Zilioli's entry is included in Elisa Innocenzi Greggio, p. 65 on. This early biographer made much of Stampa's numerous courters and admirers, whom she mocked, and the freedom of her life. Naturally, this added fuel to Salza's fire.

3. "Gaspara Stampa," in *Nuovo dizionario istorico* (Napoli: Flauto, 1794), XXIV, 393.

4. See Eugenio Donadoni, *Gaspara Stampa* (Messina, 1919), pp. 43–45, for more information on fictional and dramatic works based on the poet's life or pseudobiography and Maria Bandini Buti, *Poetesse e scrittrici,* Enciclopedia Biografica Serie 6 e Bibliografia "Italiana," 2 vols. (Roma: Istituto Editoriale Italiano, 1941), II, 282–83. In her entry on "Gaspara Stampa," Bandini Buti offers an extensive bibliography on the poet, including articles, newspaper accounts, fictional works, and plays. It is an excellent resource tool for finding information on early twentieth-century and nineteenth-century materials.

5. Using documentation he had unearthed, Salza tried to demonstrate that, given her free life, general education, some unsavory friends, and an uncertain income, Stampa was inevitably a courtesan. Salza's evidence is damaging but hardly conclusive. The most significant proofs are two poems.

One is a *mot d'esprit* by Speroni (a Stampian acquaintance), in the nature of a limerick; he compares two musical sisters—Gaspara and Cassandra—on the basis of their artistry and their being *landra* ("whores"), an obvious play on the rhyme -andra. The value of this proof is disputable: it is uncertain, although probable, that the two musicians were the Stampa sisters and, even if it were they, it was common in the Renaissance for even the most upstanding ladies to be defamed. More damaging evidence is provided by the famous libelous sonnet. This poem is posthumous, supposedly the last in a series of such slanderous works directed against Stampa. The author is unknown, as is the exact date of composition, although presumably after the publication of the *Rime* in 1554, since it is an obvious parody of one of Gaspara's own sonnets. This rather obscene composition calls the poet "a queen among whores," states that the man who deflowered her was a certain Gritti, and adds that her greatest pleasure was copulation. It also declares that Stampa lived by thievery, plagiarized her poetry, and died as a result of sexual excess. Besides the offensive language, the tone itself is virulent, all of which might tend to make its content's veracity questionable. It is interesting to note that Salza accepted all the sexual elements as truthful, but rejected the suggestions of criminal and literary larceny.

6. Bandello mentions Caterina da San Celso a number of times in his short stories. Apparently her marriage had caused considerable scandal among the members of polite society. His description of her is an indicator of the qualities respected and criticized in a lady of the sixteenth century: "She was very beautiful, being big rather than small, pretty, graceful, charming, and better-read than you might think. She played, sang, acted, and composed sweet and pleasant compositions in our vulgar tongue. She also entertained every great prince with exceptional grace, and the more one frequented her, the more amiable and gracious she became. But because she was—as is public knowledge—not very decent, she was considered neither admirable nor dear. Nor do these indecent women harm only themselves, but they also give people reason to murmur about their relatives, husbands, and children, making their lives unhappy" (Matteo Bandello, I, 445).

7. The term *cortigiana* was—to quote Bandello—an "honest word." It is the feminine of *cortigiano*, "the courtier," and derives from the word *corte*, "court." It is certainly a more elevated expression than *puttana* or *meretrice*, common words for a prostitute or whore. Bandello also gives an amusing description of the life of the Venetian *cortigiana* in his stories. It was the custom, it appears, for her to have six or seven gentleman callers who had an appointed night each week to dine with his mistress and share her bed. Her

days were thus free for "those who come and go," and she might trade off days for nights in case a foreigner with a "well-furnished purse" might appear. For these services, she was paid a monthly salary, with the understanding she would be free to entertain foreigners days (cf. Matteo Bandello, II, 417–18).

8. An informative and enjoyable book on the Italian courtesans, including Veronica Franco, is Georgina Masson's *Courtesans of the Italian Renaissance* (London: Secker and Warburg, 1975). Although dozens of famous sixteenth-century *hetaerae* are discussed, Gaspara Stampa is not among them.

9. The most recent rejection of Salza's theory appears in Maria Bellonci's "Introduzione" to the newest edition of the *Rime* (Milano, 1976), pp. 5–25. Bellonci herself has done considerable research and written a number of books on women in the Renaissance.

10. The first quotation is from Benedetto Croce, *Conversazioni Critiche,* 2nd ed. (Bari, 1924), p. 225; the second is taken from Croce's *Poesia popolare e poesia d'arte,* 2nd ed. (Bari, 1946), pp. 366–67.

11. Donadoni, p. 41.

12. Reichenbach captures the tone of this romantic defense in the conclusion of his opus on the poet. Conceding the possible validity of Salza's opinions, he adds: ". . . for all that, this mysterious and fascinating figure would not precipitate from her pedestal into the mud. No, whatever the depressing events and sadness of her life were, there is in this woman a fervor, a passion, an emotional impetus that redeems her and saves her; the more her wretched flesh humbles itself under the merciless gaze of history, the more her soul, delirious with heaven, stands out. And the anguished cry of her love grips us all the more when we feel that this love is condemned from birth, like the flight of an eagle with a wounded wing." Giulio Reichenbach, *Gaspara Stampa* (Roma, 1923), p. 57.

13. Bandello, I, 481.

14. Donadoni, pp. 94–95, 97. The quotation from Ada Negri was taken from Salza, "Madonna Gasparina Stampa secondo nuove indagini," p. 58.

15. Justin Vitiello, "Gaspara Stampa: The Ambiguities of Martyrdom," *Modern Language Notes* 90 (January 1975): 66. Vitiello presents a perceptive portrait of what he terms Stampa's "critical ambiguity," the ironic twist whereby the poet humbles herself only to exalt herself and her art, in pp. 65–71.

16. For detailed information on Abdelkader Salza's reordering of the *Rime,* see the "Nota" to Gaspara Stampa and Veronica Franco, *Rime,* pp.

367–73. Salza's decision to close the *canzoniere* with Stampa's poetry of religious contrition was arbitrary, but it does give a forceful conclusion to the work, ending it on a spiritual and poignant note.

Chapter Three

1. For more information on Pietro Bembo's influence on poetry and his role in the *questione della lingua* and his views on imitation see Luigi Baldacci, "Pietro Bembo: dal *De Imitatione* alle *Prose,*" in *Il Petrarchismo italiano nel Cinquecento* (Milano: Ricciardi, 1957), pp. 1–32; W. Theodore Elwert, "Pietro Bembo e la vita letteraria del suo tempo," in *La civiltà veneziana del Rinascimento* (Firenze: Sansoni, 1958), pp. 127–76; Roccò Montano, *Estetica del Rinacimento e del Barocco* (Napoli: Quaderni di Delta, 1962); Giorgio Santangelo, *Il Petrarchismo del Bembo e di altri poeti del '500* (Roma: Istituto Editoriale Cultura Europea, 1962); and Ettore Bonora, "Pietro Bembo," in *Storia della letteratura italiana: Il Cinquecento,* eds. Emilio Cecchi and Natalino Sapegno (Milano: Garzanti, 1965), pp. 156–72.

2. Toward the end of 1512, Bembo wrote an epistle to Giovan Francesco Pico which picked up on the disputes on style already in progress. In this work he states the need for a sole model of excellence. *De imitatione* [On Imitation] suggests, as suitable models for Latin, the prose writer Cicero and the poet Virgil. The passage from a Latin to a vernacular model was an easy one for Bembo to make, once the need for an adequate style to express the writer's content was established.

3. Salvatore Battaglia and Giancarlo Mazzacurati, *La letteratura italiana: Rinascimento e Barocco* (Firenze: Sansoni, 1974), p. 101.

4. For more information on the definition and uses of imitation in the Cinquecento, consult Joel Spingarn, *A History of Literary Criticism in the Renaissance* (New York: Harcourt Brace and World, 1963). This book has undergone a number of editions and printings, the first being 1899, and the second 1908. For a definition of the contrasting views of imitation in Italy, see "Il principio dell'imitazione nelle polemiche dei letterati italiani durante il Rinascimento," in Santangelo, pp. 27–54.

5. Logan, p. 101.

6. Cf. Burke, pp. 123–44. The quotation in the text is from p. 135.

7. Giacinto Spagnoletti, *Il Petrarchismo* (Milano: Garzanti, 1959), pp. 18–19.

8. See Baldacci, "Il Petrarca specchio di vita," pp. 45–74.

9. The final tercet of this poetic epitaph reads: "Traveler, pray for her rest and peace and learn from her, so ill-used, to never follow a cruel and

fleeting heart." This particular poem was used by Stampa's vituperative contemporary to compose the infamous sonnet on which Salza based much of the evidence for his thesis. It is a direct paraphrase, which initiates: "Traveler, stop if you wish to know the outcome of my wretched life: I was Gaspara Stampa. . . ."

10. The following sonnets also have discernible Petrarchan echoes, and a similar type of comparative and contrasting analysis between original and imitation can be undertaken: "Vieni, Amor, a veder la gloria mia" (Stampa, LI) and Petrarca's "Stiamo, Amore, a veder la gloria nostra" (CXCII); "Io pur aspetto, e non veggo che giunga" (Stampa, XCIX) and "I' pur ascolto, e non odo novella" (CCLIV), both of which deal with the tardy arrival of news from the beloved; "S'io 'l dissi mai, signor, che mi sia tolto" (Stampa, CXXVIII) and the Petrarchan anaphora "S'i' 'l dissi mai, ch'i' vegna in odio a quella," both based on the Provençal *escondig*, or poem of defense; Stampa's Adriatic, "O rive, o lidi, che già foste porto" (CXL), replaces Petrarca's little room of "O cameretta che già fosti un porto" (CCXXXIV). These are among the most evident borrowings binding Gaspara Stampa to the Petrarchan model, but a close comparative reading of the two *canzonieri* will result in numerous others which are less obvious, being often limited to a few allusive words within a composition, or a suggestive rhythm. It must be remembered that Petrarca was in the public domain; his expressions were as common in certain circles as some publicity jingles are today.

11. Fortunato Rizzi, *L'anima del Cinquecento e la lirica volgare* (Milano: Fratelli Treves, 1928), p. 42.

12. Cf. Luigi Malagoli, "La nuova sensibilitá e il nuovo stile: Gaspara Stampa," in *Le contraddizioni del Rinascimento* (Firenze, 1968), pp. 108–109.

13. The term "plurality" is borrowed from Giulio Ferroni, *Poesia italiana del Cinquecento* (Milano: Garzanti, 1978), pp. ix–xi. The term seems eminently suited to these stylistic structures.

14. In the Renaissance, Venice was one of the few areas where Protestants were welcome and unharassed and where Catholic reformers were given a fair amount of freedom of religion and thought. These groups also did much of their devotional and propagandistic publishing in the city, where the numerous printing presses were available to all. Stampa was doubtlessly aware of the reformist currents both because of the great numbers of foreigners in the city who participated in its social entertainments and because of the traditional freedom of expression associated with the Venetian atmosphere. Lutherans were especially numerous in the city and the poet probably heard a great deal about their dogma after the split with the Catholic Church of

Rome. Nothing is really known of Stampa's own religious beliefs and views, however.

15. The religious sonnets that close the *Rime* borrow heavily from the Petrarchan model. CCCV is derived from *Canzoniere* CCCLXV, "I' vo' piangendo. . .," in its regret for having wasted precious time in loving mortal things rather than celestial objects and in its plea for divine intercession. God's "giving a hand" to the penitent sinner is an image used by both poets. Besides the unity of themes, the language is also derivative, as is to be expected. Stampa's "Mesta e pentita" echoes the situation of Petrarca's "Padre del ciel" (LXIII); both emphasize the word *vaneggiar*, an elusive expression which can signify vanities, mortal or material objects, but also the fantasizing associated with both loving and writing poetry.

Chapter Four

1. John Charles Nelson, *Renaissance Theory of Love* (New York: Columbia University Press, 1958), p. 69.

2. Cf. Giuseppe Toffanin, *Storia letteraria d'Italia: Il Cinquecento,* 7th ed. (Milano, 1927/1965), p. 137.

3. Bembo's emphasis on the number three is, naturally, not casual. Historically, the number three is symbolic of the Trinity and reflects the attainment of perfection. Within the framework of *Gli Asolani* the number indicates the fusion of the other two types of love (the painful and the joyous) into the perfect spiritual love exalted during the third conversation. Within a literary context, Bembo is alluding to the two great works of Dante, *La vita nuova* (itself the story of a love first misinterpreted and then spiritualized) and the *Divine Comedy* (in which man ascends to God, total perfection), as well as to the entire Italian poetic tradition. By using the three, Bembo is able to blend theology, literary history, and Platonism.

4. For more details see the chapter titled "Gli *Asolani* del Bembo e Venere celeste," in Baldacci, pp. 86–114, which discusses not only Bembo's work but the influence of Platonism on Petrarca, Leone Ebreo, Castiglione, and others.

5. Nelson, p. 90. Nelson's book has an excellent discussion of the various love treatises of the Italian Renaissance in Chapter 2, pp. 67–162. Also see Ettore Bonora, "La lirica e i trattati d'amore," in *Critica e letteratura del Cinquecento* (Torino, 1964), pp. 55–91; Crane, pp. 108–46; Nesca A. Robb, *Neoplatonism of the Italian Renaissance* (London: G. Allen & Unwin Ltd. 1935); and the sixth chapter of Giuseppe Toffanin's work. As for the love treatises themselves, most are contained in Zonta's book *Trattati d'amore*

del '500, reprinted by Laterza in 1975. The collection includes Giuseppe Betussi's *Il Raverta* and *La Leonora*, Francesco Sansovino's *Ragionamento d'amore*, Tullia d'Aragona's *De la infinità di amore*, and Bartolomeo Gottifredi's *Specchio d'amore*. All are in dialogue form, following the Platonic model.

6. Vitiello, p. 62.

7. See Luigi Russo, "Gaspara Stampa e il Petrarchismo del '500," *Belfagor* 13, Fascicolo 1 (31 gennaio 1958): 9-13.

8. Quoted by Baldacci, p. 92.

Chapter Five

1. Cf. Luigi Baldacci, "Gaspara Stampa," in *Lirici del Cinquecento* (Firenze, 1957), p. 103.

2. Walter Binni, "Gaspara Stampa," in *Critici e poeti dal Cinquecento al Novecento* (Firenze, 1951), p. 14. Besides Binni, Ettore Bonora also discusses the musicality of Stampa's poetry in "Le donne poetesse," in *Critica e letteratura*, pp. 102-107. As for her ties with the Arcadia, Gaspara Stampa occasionally lends herself to such a comparison. The Arcadians had emphasized a return to the bucolic life of shepherds and shepherdesses, seeking a simplicity greatly lacking in the eighteenth century. They even assumed pastoral names upon entering one of the Arcadian groups, or clubs. The Arcadian experience seems quite close to Stampa's own in the Accademia dei Dubbiosi, or in another similar circle in Venice, when she took on the name of Anassilla and wrote poetry to her friends, the shepherds, who honored her. Gaspara's experience was both brief and limited, whereas the Arcadia invaded all of Italy in the Settecento, but the resemblances are striking. There are a few sonnets where Stampa joins the pastoral imagery and simplicity to the songlike quality associated with the melodrama's *ariette* (little arias or songs) or the *canzonette*, in vogue during the eighteenth century. The poetry in which she assumes the identity of Anassilla tends to be set in nature, often along the shores of the Adriatic—hardly typical of shepherds!—which seem to be a constant emblem of peace or freedom in contrast to the urban setting of Venice. It is from this uninhabited atmosphere, dominated by sea, shore, wind, and sun, that the protagonist "calls out to her shepherd" who is absent. The message, or rather song, is in harmony with both the setting and the pastoral character of Anassilla: "—È questa quella viva e salda fede,/che promettevi a la tua pastorella,/quando, partendo a la stagion novella,/n'andasti ove 'l gran re gallico siede?" ("Is this that deep and steady faith

you promised your little shepherdess when, leaving her in the spring, you left
to go where the great Gallic king resides?") (CCI).

3. Giovanni Macchia, "Quattro poetesse del Cinquecento," *Rivista
Rosminiana di Filosofia e di Cultura* 31 (1937): 154.

4. Malagoli, p. 116.

5. Ibid., p. 110. Malagoli has a long and detailed analysis of Stampa's
use of the hyperbole, seeing this rhetorical device as a symbol of the historical
crisis facing the Renaissance. The loss of order, measure, proportion, and
stability in life is reflected in the exaggeration and distortions of the
hyperbole, which mirrors man's lack of inner harmony through language. In
fact, Stampa's tendency to overstatement is a prognostication of the excesses
and artifice of the Baroque.

6. This sonnet was partially quoted by Gabriele D'Annunzio in his
popular and decadent novel, *Il fuoco* (1900), contributing to the legendary
interpretation of the poet's life and works. The hero says of the poet's verse,
"it is a mixture of intense cold and fierce heat," an antithesis Gaspara Stampa
would have appreciated.

Selected Bibliography

PRIMARY SOURCES

The following is a chronological list of the main editions and publications of Gaspara Stampa's only work, the *Rime*. A brief description of its features and contents will be added to each entry.

Rime di Madonna Gaspara Stampa. Edited by Giorgio Benzone and Cassandra Stampa. Venice: Pietrasanta, 1554. Includes the poetry, the dedication to Monsignor Giovanni Della Casa written by Cassandra, a few sonnets in honor of the poet's death, and Gaspara's own dedication to Collaltino di Collalto.

Rime di Madonna Gaspara Stampa con alcune altre di Collaltino e di Vinciguerra conti di Collalto, e di Baldassare Stampa. Edited by Luisa Bergalli and Apostolo Zeno. Venice: Piacentini, 1738. As the title makes clear, this second edition includes poetry by Gaspara and Baldassare Stampa, as well as the two Collalto brothers. This collection is not faithful in full to the original. It has biographical sketches of all the poets, penned by Antonio Rambaldo di Collalto, rich illustrations, and a large number of poems in honor of the poet(s) composed by some eighteenth-century Arcadians.

Rime di Gaspara Stampa nuovamente pubblicate. Edited by Pia Mestica Chiappetti. Florence: Barbera, 1877. Includes a "Life of Gaspara Stampa" by the editor and undertakes some orthographic changes.

Rime di tre gentildonne del secolo XVI: Vittoria Colonna, Gaspara Stampa, Veronica Gambara. Edited by Olindo Guerrini. Milano: Sonzogno, 1882. Follows Mestica Chiappetti's publication.

Rime di Gaspara Stampa e di Veronica Franco. Edited by Abdelkader Salza. Bari: Laterza, 1913. The only critical edition of Stampa's poetry, based on the 1554 edition. Includes poetry by Baldassare Stampa, Collaltino and Vinciguerra di Collalto, sonnets in honor of the poet, and a "Nota," in which the editor discusses his methodology.

Le più belle pagine di Gaspara Stampa, Vittoria Colonna, Veronica Gambara, Isabella di Morra. Milano: Treves, 1935. Compiled by Giuseppe

Toffanin, who adds an introduction, this is an anthology. The editor
also alters the sequence of the poems, so that the story of Gaspara's love
for Collaltino shows up.

Rime. Edited by Rodolfo Ceriello. Milano: Rizzoli, 1954. Issued on the
400th anniversary of the poet's death, it includes notes.

Rime. Milano: Rizzoli, 1976. Includes an introduction by Maria Bellonci, a
chronology, a description of the various editions, and a summary of
Stampa's relation to literary criticism, as well as a selected bibliography,
and some "Documenti." Ceriello's notes to the 1954 edition become
footnotes. These last two publications of the *Rime* follow Salza's edition
to the letter.

SECONDARY SOURCES

Baldacci, Luigi. "Gaspara Stampa." In *Lirici del Cinquecento.* Florence:
Salani, 1957, pp. 102–108. Discusses Stampa's ability to reject the
rhetorical experience of her contemporaries in order to find a spontaneous mode of personal expression.

Bandini Buti, Maria. "Gaspara Stampa," *Poetesse e scrittrici,* Vol. II, 278–
83, in *Enciclopedia Biografica Serie 6 e Bibliografia "Italiana".* Roma:
Istituto Editoriale Italiano, 1941. A lengthy if not totally accurate
encyclopedic entry, followed by an extensive bibliography of eighteenth-
and early nineteenth-century materials.

Bassanese, Fiora A. "The Feminine Voice: Gaspara Stampa." *Canadian
Journal of Italian Studies* 3, no. 2 (Winter 1980):81–88.

Bellonci, Maria. "Introduzione" to *Rime.* By Gaspara Stampa. Milano:
Rizzoli, 1976, pp. 5–25. An excellent overview of the poet and the
poetry from a slightly feminist angle.

Binni, Walter. "Gaspara Stampa." In *Critici e poeti dal Cinquecento al
Novecento.* Florence: La Nuova Italia, 1951, pp. 3–16. One of the best
articles available on Stampa's poetry, placing it in the context of
Petrarchismo but noting its originality and musical qualities.

Bonora, Ettore. "Le donne poetesse." In *Critica e letteratura nel Cinquecento.*
Torino: Giappichelli, 1964, pp. 93–110. The same article is included
in *Storia della letteratura italiana: Il Cinquecento.* Edited by Emilio
Cecchi and Natalino Sapegno. Milano: Garzanti, 1966, pp. 241–58.
Considers the poet's musical qualities, especially in the madrigals,
emphasizing the elegiac elements of her compositions.

Borgese, G. A. "Il processo di Gaspara Stampa." In *Studi di letterature moderne.* Milano: Treves, 1915, pp. 20–28. One of the principal articles written in defense of Stampa against Salza. The poet is viewed as somewhere between Petrarca and Goethe's *Werther.*

Brognoligo, Gioachino. "Gaspara Stampa." *Giornale storico della letteratura italiana* 76 (1920):134–45. An intelligent analysis of the views of Donadoni and Cesareo on Gaspara Stampa and on the Salza controversy.

Carrer, Luigi. "Gaspara Stampa." In *Anello di sette gemme o Venezia e la sua storia.* Venice: Gondolieri, 1838. Also published as *Amore infelice di Gaspara Stampa* in 1851, this work is an epistolary novel, or "fantasy" as Carrer himself suggests. The prime example of the Romantics' desire to create a myth of Stampa the woman.

Cesareo, G. A. *Gaspara Stampa donna e poetessa.* Napoli: Perrella, 1920. A major document in the biographical dispute. Cesareo opposes Salza with vehemence if a bit of naiveté.

Croce, Benedetto. *Conversazioni critiche.* 2nd ed. Bari: Laterza, 1924, pp. 223–33. A distinction between the real and the fantastic Stampa is made in light of the biographical polemics, with an invitation to return to the poetry.

———. *Poesia popolare e poesia d'arte.* 2nd ed. Bari: Laterza, 1946, pp. 366–75. A survey of the *Rime* as an epistolary or diary or confession.

De Benedetti, F. Augusto. "La poesia di Gaspara Stampa." *Rassegna Nazionale* 34, Serie II (1936):210–16. A book review of Toffanin's *Le più belle pagine.*

Di Pino, Guido. "Veronica Gambara-Gaspara Stampa." In *Atteggiamenti e figure della lirica del Cinquecento.* Messina-Florence: D'Anna, 1958, pp. 133–52. A stylistic analysis emphasizing the formal characteristics of Stampa's prosody, in opposition to the declaration that the poetry is little more than an epistolary in verse.

Dolci, Giulio. "Gaspara Stampa." In *Letteratura italiana: I Minori.* Milano: Marzorati, 1961, II, 315–25. A general introduction.

Donadoni, Eugenio. *Gaspara Stampa.* Messina: Principato, 1919. Donadoni attempts to solve the biographical dispute by defining her as an *irregolare.* A rather complete and balanced overview of the poet's biography, the critical polemics, and the *Rime* as poetry.

Innocenzi Greggio, Elisa. "In difesa di Gaspara Stampa." *L'Ateneo Veneto* 38 (1915):1–158. After Salza's articles, the best piece of historical criticism and documentation available on Stampa the historical figure.

Macchia, Giovanni. "Quattro poetesse del Cinquecento." *Rivista Rosminiana di Filosofia e di Cultura* 31 (1937):152–57. A review of Toffanin's *Le più belle pagine,* emphasizing Stampa's poetical effusions.

Malagoli, Luigi. "La nuova sensibilità e il nuovo stile: Gaspara Stampa." In *Le contraddizioni del Rinascimento.* Florence: La Nuova Italia, 1968, pp. 105–23. Also published in similar form as *La Lirica del Cinquecento e Gaspara Stampa.* Pisa: Libreria Golliardica, 1966. A most comprehensive analysis of Stampa's poetry. The author chooses Stampa and Michelangelo as the representatives of a historical-social metamorphosis in progress, which is expressed in their style.

Neri, Ferdinando. "Le rime ultime di Gaspara Stampa." In *Saggi di letteratura italiana francese inglese.* Naples: Loffredo, 1936, pp. 269–73. A superficial look at the *Rime* as the document of a fervent passion.

Pancrazi, Pietro. "I due romanzi di Gasparina." In *Nel giardino di Candido.* Florence: Le Monnier, 1950, pp. 127–32. The two "novels" are the one depicted in the *Rime* and the other created by the poet's biographers and critics.

Pirotti, Ugo. "Sulle *Rime* di Gaspara Stampa." *Convivium,* No. 6 (1948):848–61. A survey of the critical polemics and an analysis of the poet's style and novel voice.

Reichenbach, Giulio. *Gaspara Stampa.* Roma: Formiggini, 1923. A descriptive, semibiographical reading of the *Rime,* with a summation of the critical dispute, emphasizing Stampa's passionality and sincerity.

Russo, Luigi. "Gaspara Stampa e il Petrarchismo del '500." *Belfagor* 13, Fascicolo 1 (31 gennaio 1958):1–20. A comprehensive and unbiased study of Stampa's Petrarchismo.

Salza, Abdelkader. "Madonna Gasparina Stampa secondo nuove indagini." *Giornale storico della letteratura italiana* 62 (1913):1–101, and "Madonna Gasparina Stampa e la società veneziana del suo tempo." *GSLI* 70 (1917):1–60, 281–99. The most comprehensive historical and documentary study done. The critic proposes that Stampa was a courtesan, in contrast to prevailing romantic opinion. The second article rebuts the arguments presented by his opposition and presents more documentation.

Toffanin, Giuseppe. "Le donne poetesse e Michelangelo." In *Storia letteraria d'Italia: Il Cinquecento.* 7th ed. Milano: Vallardi, 1927/1965. An overview, emphasizing the complex psychological content of the *Rime.*

Vitiello, Justin. "Gaspara Stampa: The Ambiguities of Martyrdom." *Modern Language Notes* (January 1975):58–71. A perceptive and detailed analysis of three exemplary Stampian sonnets.

Index

DATE DUE
